Ducksoup
The Wisdom of Simple Cooking

Clare Lattin and Tom Hill

CHRONICLE BOOKS
SAN FRANCISCO

Introduction

My friend Georgia Bateman and I were having lunch at Ducksoup recently and she kept making those noises you make when something is just so tasty. She didn't say much throughout lunch because she was so busy wolfing it down. When she'd finished she looked at me and said, "God, I just love food that makes me make those noises." For me that sums up what we do at Ducksoup: we make food that makes you make those noises—they are the sound of deliciousness.

Cooking can be so many different things, but for us it's about using just a few simple seasonal ingredients and turning them into something more than the sum of their parts. The Japanese have an expression called *kokumi*—a compound of the words for "rich" and "taste." But it's as much a feeling as it is a taste, and it's often described as a sense of "thickness" or "mouthfeel." *Kokumi* is not an independent taste like umami, but it does imply taste enhancement and is associated with food that is truly delicious. And I suppose it was all those things that Georgia was experiencing when she was making those sounds. We're not in any way Japanese at Ducksoup, but we are trying to achieve something along the lines of what *kokumi* means.

Opening a restaurant was never part of life's plan, but when I reflect, I realize it was my calling. I am obsessive about good food, wine, and the experiences I have around them. I love to cook, and like anyone who enjoys cooking, it's the process that gets me, like directing your own little theater production. I also love the security it offers you and those around you: that all is well with the world. The satisfaction of giving a little piece of yourself through your food is a very rewarding experience. I don't think there are many things that can come close to sharing a good meal with people you care about.

And that's how it is at Ducksoup, the restaurant I opened with friends in London's Soho back in September 2011. It's a tiny place with a menu that changes weekly, closely following the seasons. We all feel very connected to our customers, as though they're our extended family, and we feel a similar satisfaction from feeding them as we do our own friends and family.

Our approach to cooking is about ingredients (or essentially flavor) and simplicity. It's about knowing when ingredients are at their best, and understanding how the use of their flavors or textures is going to transform something from standard to outstanding in the simplest way possible. Some pasta in the pantry, sage or rosemary growing at the back door, some Parmesan and good olive oil, and in a matter of minutes you've got something deeply satisfying and delicious on your plate. Minimal ingredients, little cooking, and maximum flavor: it's a method we like to follow as much as we can.

Every Friday at the restaurant, Tom and I sit down together and talk about food. Not in any specific way—we just share our thoughts about ingredients, what's in season, and what we're in the mood to eat, and ideas often grow out of that. It's important for us that what we cook is based around our own stories and experiences, because it means that so much more soul and understanding go into the dish. The simplicity of how we cook means the dishes often evoke something familiar and innate in both ourselves and our customers. This is because much of our food is inspired by a dish we cook at home, something we've had while traveling, or even something we've imagined eating.

Once you've cooked a few recipes from this book, you'll quickly become familiar with how we cook using our "larder" essentials: the things we come back to time and time again. We like to think of them as our natural flavor enhancers. A squeeze of burnt lemon, a sprinkling of fried curry leaves, a handful of toasted nuts—these simple things have the power to transform a dish.

Keeping things really simple means that we often describe our menu as being "clean." We want our food to taste of itself, so we do little to it. We don't wrap it up in butter or sauces, but just add a gentle seasoning or an ingredient that will help it become a better version of itself. We try to think of each little ensemble as a group of people all going out together; we think of how they might get along, who might be the leader, who might be the enabler—that sort of thing. Of course, the ideal situation is when each ingredient supports and nurtures the others, so they become more bold and confident in flavor.

Without good ingredients it's not easy to achieve the above. Seasonal produce or ingredients that have been lovingly produced or grown means they will be full of flavor; when you have these, you're

halfway there. We use a lot of vegetables in our cooking—this isn't because we're catering to vegetarians, it's simply how things have developed over time. The flavor pairings we use in these dishes are so delicious that we haven't felt the need to use as much meat. However, don't be alarmed if you like meat; there are plenty of recipes in this book that use it.

I suppose we have quite a magpie approach to cooking and draw on a palette of ingredients inspired by our travels—whether Italian, Middle Eastern, Spanish, or Nordic. We use the best ingredients from different places, and because our style of cooking is so free, these recipes are very easily re-created at home.

We like to think of our menus as a journal of what we want to eat. In short, it's simple, humble cooking, using minimal ingredients and lively flavor pairings. This book is a snapshot of those dishes, the ones we think work well for the home cook. And we hope that you'll love using these recipes.

Hungry Beginnings

I was a child with an insatiable appetite. It was the '70s, and good food was a luxury, olive oil was something sold in a tiny bottle at the local chemist, and avocados were the height of sophistication. We had them once in a while and, like everyone back then, my mother would keep the pits in glasses of water on the windowsills, in the hope that they would become more plentiful.

I was always hungry and would eat dried spaghetti, tear off corners of Jello packets or scour the cupboards for escapee currants. When it came to dessert, I was so scared that my brother and sister would get more than me that my mother would have to get out the scale and weigh each portion. I'd oversee the procedure and choose the one weighing the most—but even then I didn't trust the scale and ended up choosing by sight. At three years old, I used to demolish jars of Greek olives and loved my father's coq au vin and my mother's curry. When I look back, perhaps it's no surprise that I have found myself in the world of food and restaurants.

I began my career in publishing, which is how I met Mark Hix. We had a shared passion for food and restaurants, and it was his dream to open a restaurant of his own. In 2005 the Hix Oyster & Chop House became a reality, and I was able to experience the inner workings of a restaurant firsthand—the passion and dedication required was addictive. It was there that I met Tom Hill and Rory McCoy (who I would later end up in business with at Ducksoup) and, later, Julian Biggs. Both Mark and Julian taught me so much through their approach to simple seasonal cooking. When Tom finally joined Ducksoup it was clear that he also shared the same vision. It is a wonderful thing to share a similar approach to food and cooking.

Travels

I've been lucky enough to travel to some wonderful places, but it was while visiting the Middle East with Julian that my eyes were really opened to the many ingredients and flavors we use in the restaurant today.

Back in 2009 the inner city of Damascus, nestled behind decaying walls, held a subtle magic. The tiny hole-in-the-wall spaces with ingenious ways of cramming in as many people as possible, the tables that folded down, or up, the plastic crates of juice bottles piled from floor to ceiling that doubled as seats—all took a hold over me.

The presence of food vendors as a necessity—rather than food as part of entertainment as it so often is back home—really appealed to me. I loved the simple, down-to-earth places that served good food in a straightforward, easy environment. Practicality and well-prepared food were the only two things at work, and nothing else mattered.

This felt like a big contrast to London, where even just a few years ago, eating out still involved much ceremony or occasion. Restaurants would put so much effort into making things pristine and perfect, which often rendered the dishes bland and characterless. The option of dining out alone seemed more difficult then, too. Having to wait two weeks for a friend to become available so that you could go try a new restaurant was frustrating. Things are very different now in London, of course. The London food scene has since become much more diverse across the whole spectrum, from fine dining to street food. But back then Damascus felt like a whole other world. When I came home I craved a more accessible way of eating out, one without the formality. I love eating alone in restaurants and ordering exactly what I want. I wanted to create a place where you could eat straightforwardly good food and be home at a reasonable hour, watered and fed without drama or fuss.

Damascus opened my eyes to some of the most exotic ingredients, sounds, and smells—of intoxicating spices and gardens billowing with the scents of rose and orange blossom. I remember buying a bottle of pure orange blossom oil from the market. It leaked into my bag on my way home, and for months after returning I wafted the scent of orange blossom wherever I went, to the point of embarrassment—it was that potent.

These flavors are all present in our cooking at Ducksoup. We often use za'atar, a blend of oregano, sesame seeds, and sumac, to add a zesty bite to salads and vegetables. We enhance drinks and desserts with orange blossom and rose water. Tahini yogurt is by far one of our biggest "go-to" dressings, added with a sprinkling of dukkah (a mix of spices, herbs, and nuts) to complete any number of dishes.

Beirut was another Middle Eastern destination that felt exciting, exotic, edgy, and perhaps slightly forbidden after its troubles. I'd read about an emerging food scene and was keen to experience it, so my good friend Anissa Helou, who was born in Beirut, took me to a café owned by Kamal Mouzawak, who was working with local farmers to present their food in a more interesting way. It was a colorful and lively place with no designated table plan—you just showed up, took your food, sat down, and ate and chatted with whomever you found yourself next to: a truly democratic and convivial way to dine. I flashed back to London, thinking of those restaurants that lined up row upon row of tables for two, and my heart sank.

Beirut is full of hidden gems and one of the most curious cities I've visited. The people are immensely hospitable and passionate about their heritage. Anissa took us to a local restaurant in the Armenian quarter, where we ate a dish of lots of tiny birds. It reminded me of the time when Mark and I cooked tiny birds for Christmas lunch. We all put napkins over our heads as we sucked out the brains. This culinary tradition comes from France, where the feasting on songbirds was long considered the pinnacle of gastronomic delight. Some say the napkin helps the diner savor the aroma; others say that it is intended to conceal your greed from God. Neither the aroma nor the eye of God seemed to bother the Armenians; they were

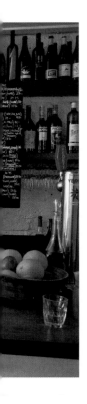

happy to pick, chew, and suck for all to see. When in Beirut . . . But the contrast between the traditional French formality and a more informal approach lingered in my mind long after I got back.

Another amazingly passionate person was Naylor Audi, who is renowned for having the best ice cream shop in central Beirut, with a wild menagerie of flavors and textures full of mastic (the gum that gives Middle Eastern ice cream its unique chew). Naylor introduced me to freekeh, which is wheat that is harvested while still green and then carefully burned to give it a subtle and delicious smokiness. We now use this as one of our "go-to" grains, and it's gaining popularity today for its high nutritional content.

From Beirut we went on to Lebanon's second city, Tripoli, with Cherine Yazbeck, author of *The Rural Taste of Lebanon*. Tripoli was an eye-opener; the entire city seemed to epitomize the democracy of eating. Here were a bunch of people cooking whatever it is that they specialize in and serving it in completely unpretentious surroundings. I was becoming more and more obsessed with the idea of serving good food in an accessible environment without fuss or ceremony.

Ducksoup takes so many of its features, both slight and bold, from our travels past and present. We love Nordic cuisine for its clean but strong flavors that speak directly of blue open skies, and crisp cold days. The sunbaked ingredients of Italy inspire our menu endlessly, and the aromatic warm spices of Middle Eastern cooking fill us with a longing to revisit the vibrancy of these places. When we plan our menus it always becomes a conversation about dishes we have loved eating or would love to eat. The food cultures and ingredients of far-off lands inspire us in so many ways. And, as someone obsessed with food, I plan most of my trips around how the food experience of the city or country will further influence or inspire what we do.

Other quirks, such as our handwritten shared menu, also come from such trips. Always keep your eyes and ears to the ground because there is inspiration to be had in every moment. The shared menu came about after a trip to Uruguay, in a town called La Barra, a cool, hipped-out beach town. Six of us went into a restaurant to eat lunch. When we asked for the menu, the waiter took out from his back pocket a neatly folded piece of paper. As he unfolded this tiny postcard-size piece of paper, we could see a perfect scrawl of writing, and as he handed it over to just one of us we realized this was the menu. We were expected to share and hand it back in as good condition as we'd been given it. It was a bit impractical, but what I realized is that it made everyone talk about the menu. Often when each person at the table is presented with their own menu, silence falls as everyone disappears into their own menu-reading world. I love to talk about food, and so I really enjoyed the effect this little menu had on everyone, and we adopted it at Ducksoup. Some people don't get it, and that is fine, but sometimes it's lovely to see three or four people holding a candle over the menu and discussing in detail what they are going to order.

We're often asked about our record player and vinyl, and I have Beirut to thank for this, too. We went to a tiny bar in the Gemmayzeh district with this guy sitting in the little window playing his decks and we vowed it would be a big part of what we were going to do. Just two hours before we were due to open, Rory (who I opened the restaurant with) forced me to go to Richer Sounds and get the record player I had promised we would have. "Clare, I won't open this place until there is a record on," he said. I think he had brought in *Tumbleweed Connection* by Elton John that morning and really wanted to play it! On our opening night, my friend Sue Webster donated 10 records, which she called "essentials": *Heroes* by David Bowie, *Sweet Dreams* by the Eurhythmics, *Dig Lazarus Dig* by Nick Cave and the Bad Seeds, *The Kick Inside* by Kate Bush, *Lust for Life* by Iggy Pop, *Planet Caravan* by Black Sabbath, *Shipbuilding* by Robert Wyatt, *Breaking Glass* by Hazel O'Conner, *Three Imaginary Boys* by the Cure, and *The Specials* by The Specials.

Today we have over 250 records, which is mostly thanks to Rory and his obsessiveness in searching out interesting albums. Having vinyl means that you do feel the ebb and flow of the music and the restaurant, rather than just having a never-ending playlist. And of course it means that you can play to the room, and to the exact moment of what you feel is needed. We have a lot of fun playing to different situations, such as Friday night Nirvana to late-night lovers at the bar who need to be gently reminded that it's time to go.

Something that is really important to us at Ducksoup is natural and biodynamic wine. Wine that tastes so juicy and so full of life is an obvious fit for the food that we love.

France has always been a good place to drink natural wine and find out about different producers. Tom, Rory, and I will sometimes go on day trips to Paris. We get the 7:10 from St. Pancras, which gets us into Paris in time for a slow walk over to the Canal district, where we order something in Chez Prune and wait until 12:30, when we go for lunch at Le Verre Volé, one of our favorite restaurants in Paris. Here we order a sparkling wine—whatever they recommend, as there is no wine list. You just ask what's open today or describe something you might want to drink and they talk you through a few options. I love that.

At Ducksoup we try to break through the formal and traditional way that people order wine. We have a short list of 10 wines available by the glass, which we change all the time, almost as often as our menu. We care as much about our wines as we do about our food and want customers to have new experiences. Because our wines are listed on blackboards rather than individual wine lists, most of them are sold through verbal communication. It's a relationship that customers and our staff have built up over time, and it really enhances everyone's experience as it's a much more satisfying and engaging way to work.

All these experiences have gone into creating Ducksoup, but what makes the restaurant what it is today are the personalities and passion of those who work there, creating wonderful food, selling great wine, and keeping it full of life and personality. We started out simply wanting to make good food that spoke directly about what it was: clean flavors, simple pairings, and inspiring ingredients, along with wine that shared the vibrancy of the food, served up in an environment that was straightforward and convivial. Today it is Rory McCoy and Tom Hill (both now partners in the business), Pete Dorman, Orlaith McKeever (now general manager at Rawduck, our restaurant in Hackney), and Angel Bautista who keep Ducksoup the place that it was always meant to be, making it better every day.

And So to Cooking

There are seven chapters in this book. We begin with The Ducksoup Larder, which sets out our go-to ingredients. Getting acquainted with the ingredients that are fundamental to our cooking is the best place to start. The ideas in this chapter are simple but will transform your everyday cooking. Quick Things speaks for itself: the recipes are based around just a few ingredients that can be quickly assembled, which are either raw, salted, or cured. The recipes in From the Stove use ingredients that can be quickly assembled. Recipes in A Little More Time do require this, but are dishes that can easily be enjoyed through the week. In Cooking we slow the pace down a little, with recipes that are happy with a slow afternoon "non-attention-seeking" simmer. Desserts has simple recipes that require the quick assembly of a handful of quality ingredients, as well as some that require a little more time. Finally, Preserving has recipes for pickling, salting, curing, and drinks, including a few ferments from our kitchen at Rawduck.

We have also included four short essays on things that, while not essential to your home cooking, characterize life at Ducksoup. These are On Presentation (page 81), On Charcuterie & Cheese (page 113), On Natural Wine (page 177), and On Music (page 281).

The Basics
It's always wise to read a recipe in full before you begin cooking, because there may be an element in there that you need to make in advance, such as mayonnaise, garlic, or tahini yogurt or, of course, salt cod. Not all these things take a long time, but it's best to check which things need to be prepared ahead. And you may find yourself making, for example, a batch of salt cod for a dish on the weekend and then having enough left over for another salt cod dish midweek.

There are, of course, rules in cooking, but we try not to stick to too many. However, you will see that in almost all our recipes we encourage you to taste as you go. Taste, taste, taste are our words of wisdom. Because we use so few ingredients and do so little to them, seasoning is very important; the seasoning makes the ingredient come alive. For salads we just use lemon, extra-virgin olive oil, and sea salt—we never overdress.

Don't be hesitant or scared when it comes to preheating your pan—it's really important to go all the way here and let the pan start smoking before adding your ingredient. If things are getting a little too hot, then tweak down the heat or remove the pan from the heat; as long as you remain in control things won't get out of hand.

Eating

Most of the recipes in this book can be enjoyed for lunch, a quick supper, dinner, or as part of a feast for friends and family. In fact, we've put together and photographed a feast for each season, from which you can either take elements or go whole hog—these are just ideas.

Most recipes don't require any accompaniments unless we've said so. They can simply be enjoyed with chunks of good sourdough bread, to scoop up your labneh or mop up your juices, or simply cooked potatoes or greens. All our dishes at Ducksoup are designed to be shared; with this book you'll probably find that you want to cook two or three different dishes to serve together. For this reason we have written most of the recipes to serve two, making it easier for you to adjust the quantities for larger numbers.

We're dedicated to detail in every way. Even when cooking just for yourself, presentation is something you shouldn't ignore, because it makes the meal all the better for it. If you're going to make the effort to buy and cook good food, then why not go all the way and use quirky crockery and some cloth napkins, have water or wine on the table (both is best), and use unusual bowls for sauces? Things don't have to be expensive or posh to create texture—just different. It feels good to tuck into something that looks good.

Happy cooking.

Clare Lattin, London

Here are the ingredients we come back
to time and time again when we want to
bring a fuller flavor and texture to simple
dishes. These simple larder essentials will
transform the way you cook.

The Ducksoup Larder

Go-to Ingredients

The mellowed bitter sweetness of a burnt lemon squeezed over salads or meat—no dressing required; the gentle toasting of nuts to release their oils; the vibrant zest from a sprinkling of sumac; and the sweet aromatic crunch of fried curry leaves that will transform everything in its path from good to exceptional.

At Ducksoup there are certain ingredients that we can't live without. We like to think of these as our natural flavor enhancers—the addition of tahini, the slight sourness of labneh, the garden-fresh piquancy of a green sauce, a sprinkling of sea salt, and a squeeze of lemon . . . And still there is so much more. These are the ingredients we turn to again and again—the "go-to" larder essentials that make our cooking what it is.

Because we value simplicity and always let our main ingredients speak for themselves, these larder essentials are really important. They transform the simplest of dishes into something unique and delicious. So we have fittingly devoted our first chapter to the larder. What you find here will transform the way you cook, giving you a natural feel for the ingredients and flavors that work together, and increase your confidence in the kitchen.

Organic Lemons

What other ingredient can conjure up the clean, fresh flavors of the Mediterranean as well as the lemon? Cutting through the fruit to release those zesty oils takes you straight to sunshine and endless blue skies. A salad just needs a little squeeze to lift it, lemon transforms grilled fish, and roasting lemons with meat or fish brings out their bittersweet flavor. We only use organic at Ducksoup; the fact that they are untreated means you get their natural oils when zesting.

A simple lemon dressing squeezed on almost anything

Our salads have the cleanest and most basic dressing possible: lemon juice, extra-virgin olive oil, salt. When you have good ingredients, all you need is that little lift to help their flavors come alive.

Burnt lemon

This is a great way to get a different kind of flavor from lemon. By placing a cut lemon facedown in your frying pan or roasting pan, all the natural sugars start to caramelize and burn and you end up with a lovely, sweet but still slightly tart juice. It's delicious alongside any grilled fish or meat. See page 162 for an easy dish of turmeric-spiced chickpeas, kale, garlic yogurt, and burnt lemon.

Zest

Organic lemons are a must here, as the zest has all the natural oils and flavors. Grate over mushrooms, goat's curd, warm fava beans, and prosciutto, into marinades and pasta dishes, over spring vegetables and green beans—the list is endless.

Preserved lemons

There is something very satisfying about preserving your own lemons, not least because the jars look so beautiful lined up on your shelves. They are a versatile ingredient to have on hand (you can find our recipe on page 325)—added to salads and grains or served with roasted meat, they really help to lift a dish.

Fruit curd

The minute we put this on the menu with our Brillat-Savarin cheesecake (page 299), we were reminded of the lemon curd sandwiches our mums would pack us off to school with (like a pbj in the United States). While it's not particularly healthy, it tastes just as good as it did all those years ago.

Our cheesecake wouldn't be the same without a big dollop of blood orange curd to go with it. You can find the recipe on page 301, along with other fruit toppings such as blackberries and hazelnuts and strawberry and almonds.

A Bag of Nuts

Nuts are a big feature at Ducksoup in both savory and sweet dishes, whether hazelnuts, walnuts, or almonds, dried, roasted, or wet. We usually toast them ever so slightly in a dry frying pan to bring out their natural oils. If you are toasting nuts, follow the recipe and watch them carefully, as overtoasting by just a fraction will burn the oils and you'll end up with a bitter taste.

Green almonds

When their season starts in early July we always have a big bowl of them on the bar for people to snack on. They're raw and green and have a wonderful milky texture and fresh flavor. We usually serve them with fresh ricotta and honeycomb.

Walnuts with most things

We like the way walnuts are a little more bitter than most other nuts. Crumbling them over pasta instead of using pine nuts just makes the dish a bit more wholesome. A plate of blue cheese and chicory goes well with a pile of roasted walnuts, or try the recipe for Prosciutto, Walnuts & Honey (see page 71). Buy the best quality walnuts you can afford, preferably organic, as the cheaper ones can be dry and bitter.

Hazelnuts on fish

Make a simple dressing with toasted crushed hazelnuts, lots of chopped parsley, garlic, extra-virgin olive oil, and lemon zest. It's ideal served with grilled fish or even just stirred into some pasta. Simple pleasures.

Leaves and Herbs

We use a variety of leaves and herbs throughout the year: the bitter crunch of Treviso stands up well to a soft creamy blue cheese, peppery nasturtium leaves spruce up a summer salad, and the powerful crunch of radicchio works well in salads while its flavor mellows when cooked (see our Radicchio, Gorgonzola & Hazelnut Risotto on page 189).

Bitter leaf salads

In winter you can find beautiful, bitter leaves such as radicchio and chicory. One of the prettiest that you can source from your greengrocer or farmers' market is Grumolo Verde, which is a member of the chicory family. They look like little flowers and come in pretty shades of red and green. Some of these leaves do pack a bitter note, so to ease up the flavor we pair them with a good blue cheese and lots of toasted crushed hazelnuts and—of course—lemon and oil.

Fried curry leaves

These are one of our favorite ingredients. You can buy curry leaves from good Asian grocers or online, although fresh curry leaves may not be available all year round. However, they will keep very nicely in the freezer. The oils from this leaf add an incredibly aromatic, fenugreek sweetness with a hint of citrus to your dish. We fry them in a little sunflower oil and then sprinkle them on yogurts to give the dish a magical zing. You'll find a recipe for Spring Vegetable Fritters, Cucumber Yogurt & Curry Leaves on page 169.

We also do a dish in the summer of fresh peas, pea shoots, green onions, labneh, and fried curry leaves: simply fry the green onion gently and quickly blanch the peas, then combine onions, peas, and pea shoots, spoon some labneh over them, sprinkle with your fried curry leaves and a little of the oil you cooked them in, and finish with a drizzle of olive oil.

You can do plenty more with curry leaves; don't be afraid to add them to any dish where you're using spices because they will naturally enhance the dish, and don't forget to pour that delicious infused oil you've cooked them in over the top too.

Green sauce

Green sauce is a combination of torn garden herbs, such as parsley and mint, with the addition of capers, anchovies, and olive oil. You can, of course, make it without the anchovies. It's one of those sauces that takes something from ordinary to extraordinary and is perfect spooned over grilled and roasted meats like our Grilled Poussin (see page 148), fish, or even over hot meaty braises. The trick with this sauce is to keep the leaves as chunky as you can so that you get a rustic sauce with a good texture. It's also a great way to use up any stray herbs you've got hanging around in the fridge.

SERVES 4–6

1¼ cups [15 g] flat-leaf parsley leaves
1¼ cups [15 g] mint leaves
1¼ cups [15 g] basil leaves
2 tbsp capers
2 tbsp good-quality red wine
    vinegar (we use Merlot vinegar)
1 tsp Dijon mustard
1.75 oz [50 g] salt-packed anchovies
    (about 7), chopped
Extra-virgin olive oil

Coarsely chop all the herbs, but don't chop them too finely as you want the sauce to be as chunky as possible.

Put the chopped herbs in a bowl with the capers, vinegar, mustard, and chopped anchovies and stir to combine. Slowly drizzle in just enough oil to bind all the ingredients together.

Store in the fridge in an airtight container for up to 5 days.

Greek Yogurt

When the dairy order is phoned in at the end of service, top of the list is always an 11-pound tub of Greek yogurt. We use it for so many dishes, whether as part of a sauce, a dessert, a marinade, or just a bit of cheeky staff breakfast. An 11-pound tub doesn't last us longer than a day.

Tahini yogurt

An absolute staple "go-to" accompaniment at the restaurant. We add toasted nigella and coriander seeds, garlic, and olive oil to our tahini yogurt. It works really well with a whole array of roasted vegetables (see pages 137, 156, and 167 for three recipes using tahini yogurt).

SERVES 4–6
1 tbsp coriander seeds
1 tbsp nigella seeds
Juice of ½ lemon
¼ cup [50 g] tahini paste
2 cups [500 g] thick Greek yogurt
1 garlic clove, minced
3 tbsp extra-virgin olive oil
Pinch of salt

Lightly crush the coriander seeds with a mortar and pestle and toast with the nigella seeds in a dry pan over medium heat for 5 minutes. (This wakes up the spices.)

Whisk the lemon juice and tahini together in a large bowl; it will be quite thick, but that's fine. When the seeds are toasted, add to the bowl along with all the other ingredients.

Whisk together until everything is combined. Decant into a jar or a covered bowl and store in the fridge for up to 5 days.

Garlic yogurt

By mixing Greek yogurt with lots of minced garlic, lemon juice, olive oil, and salt, you get an instant accompaniment that will go with anything grilled. One of our favorite recipes is Lamb Chops, Cumin & Garlic Yogurt (page 105).

SERVES 4–6
2 cups [500 g] thick Greek yogurt
1 garlic clove, crushed
Juice of ½ lemon
3 tbsp extra-virgin olive oil
Pinch of salt

Combine all the ingredients together in a bowl and whisk well.

Transfer to a jar or a covered bowl and store in the fridge for up to 5 days.

You can also add grated cucumber and torn mint to give the yogurt a fresher and more cooling flavor. It goes well with Spring Vegetable Fritters (page 169).

Labneh

Labneh is something we use often and make a lot of; it's an ingredient used in Middle Eastern cooking. It is salted and strained Greek yogurt, and you can find our recipe in the salting section on page 323.

Spices and Scents

Our love of Middle Eastern cooking brings spices and scents into our menus; their intoxicating and aromatic flavors can transform even the most humble of ingredients. The smell of toasted cumin and fenugreek, the airy, white, flowery aroma of orange blossom water—these are all so evocative of our travels.

Dukkah

Dukkah is a Middle Eastern blend of spices, herbs, and nuts. It's important that the nuts and seeds are evenly toasted. You can make this in large batches and store it in an airtight mason jar for up to a month, but if you leave it for longer, the flavors will begin to dull.

MAKES ABOUT 1 POUND
1 cup [150 g] toasted almonds
1 cup [150 g] toasted hazelnuts
⅓ cup [50 g] toasted sesame seeds
¼ cup [25 g] toasted coriander seeds
¼ cup [25 g] toasted cumin seeds
¼ cup [25 g] sumac
1½ tsp sea salt (we love to use Cornish sea salt)
4 tsp freshly ground black pepper
3 tbsp dried thyme

Lightly crush the almonds, hazelnuts, and seeds in a mortar and pestle and then tip into a bowl. Add the remaining ingredients and stir until well combined.

Sprinkle over a serving of Labneh under Oil (page 323) and mop up with bread. See also our recipe for Roast Eggplants, Lentils, Soft-Boiled Egg, Garlic Yogurt & Dukkah on page 165.

Sumac

Sumac is a flowering plant native to the Middle East, which produces a red berry that is dried and then ground to create a coarse powder. The flavor is tangy with a citrus element, although it's not as tart as lemon juice. Much used in Middle Eastern cooking, it's also the main component in the spice blend za'atar (see above right). We use it a lot to add a gentle zest to dishes like our Black Figs, Labneh, Pistachio & Sumac (page 65); or to simply sprinkle over grilled fish.

Za'atar

This traditional spice blend is used extensively in Middle Eastern cooking and is great sprinkled over grilled vegetables and meats like Grilled Lamb (page 215).

MAKES ABOUT 8 OUNCES
¾ cup [120 g] toasted sesame seeds
¾ cup [80 g] sumac
7 tbsp [20 g] dried oregano
Good pinch of salt

Toast your sesame seeds for 2 minutes in a dry frying pan and then combine with the remaining ingredients. Store in an airtight container for up to a month.

Rose harissa

It's much better to buy a big tub of this to keep in your fridge rather than try to create something that might not be as delicious. We use the brand Belazu, which is the best we've come across. Harissa is originally from Tunisia. Every household has a slightly different recipe for it, but the main ingredient is air-dried red chiles from North Africa, soaked and then blended with spices and garlic. All you need for a perfect meal is some good lamb (chops or boned leg) and harissa—simply coat the meat in the harissa, drizzle with oil, and grill or roast.

Breakfast is also a great time to enjoy chiles, so next time you scramble some eggs, add a teaspoon of harissa and some fresh coriander. Or you could try making one of our best-selling breakfast dishes from the brunch menu at Rawduck, our Hackney restaurant: two fried eggs on toasted sourdough, with a tablespoon (or two) of Greek yogurt, a heaping teaspoon of harissa, and a small handful of torn cilantro leaves.

♪

Urfa chile flakes

We prefer using this chile as it has a depth
of flavor rather than just heat. You can
buy it online or from most Middle Eastern
shops. It's roasted paprika that is dried in
the sun and then wrapped tightly at night
so that it sweats, infusing the dried flesh
with the remaining moisture of the pepper.
The result produces a deep color and
flavor that is less spicy than chile but with
a more intense flavor. We use it sprinkled
over grilled vegetables and meats and
with yogurt.

Rose water and orange blossom water

These are both used in traditional Middle
Eastern cooking, mainly in desserts. These
fragrant waters are distilled from the
Damascus rose and the Seville orange
tree. You can source them quite easily
these days, although it's worth doing
a little research, as there are some inferior
types out there.

Grains and Lentils

Grains play a very important role in how we cook. Our food tends to be quite vegetable-based, so it's important that we add good sources of protein and starch, which is where grains, beans, and lentils come in. Some of our favorite grains include mograbiah, fregola, and freekeh, and we also like to use Castelluccio or Puy lentils.

Mograbiah (giant couscous)

Mograbiah is a giant couscous traditionally made from bulgur wheat, hand-rolled into small balls, finely coated in wheat flour, and sun-dried. It's available online and in good supermarkets.

Fregola

Very similar in style to mograbiah; however, it's actually a type of pasta from Sardinia. Semolina dough is rolled into balls about the same size as giant couscous and toasted. You can easily find this from online suppliers.

Freekeh

Another Middle Eastern grain that is gaining popularity, not least because of its nutritional value. It's wheat that is harvested while young and green and piled up to dry in the sun. It is then carefully set on fire so that only the straw and chaff burn. The grain on the inside is too fresh to burn, and so what remains is a firm, slightly chewy grain that is nutty and smoky at the same time. We really enjoy cooking with this as a grain.

Bulgur wheat

This grain is made from cracked wheat (usually durum) that is parboiled and dried. We use it in a similar way to our other favorite grains—it has a slightly nutty taste and is also rich in nutrients.

Castelluccio and Puy lentils

These lentils are similar in style. Castelluccio are from Umbria in Italy and Puy are from south central France. Castelluccio are small and brown, while the French variety are greener in color. Both hold their shape and texture when cooked and so lend themselves to many dishes as well as a good braise.

Ricotta

Ricotta is actually a by-product of cheese-making—its name nearly means "re-cooked" in Italian. Once the milk has been separated into curds and whey and the mozzarella has been spun, the milk that is left is boiled again and strained. What you're left with is the second cheese: ricotta.

Fresh ricotta

Fresh ricotta is bought in its own muslin cloth bags and will only last a few days. Like mozzarella, it needs to be eaten young and fresh to get the most of its lovely, clean flavor.

Having a spoonful of fresh ricotta alongside a salad, grilled vegetables, or blistered tomatoes is no bad thing. Just season the top with salt and pepper, pour some olive oil over it, and enjoy. Ricotta also goes well with more explicitly salty flavors as in the recipe for Ricotta, Salted Anchovy & Toasted Buckwheat (see right).

Gnudi

Gnudi is one of those things you have to make once, because once you have you'll make it again and again—it's so good and works well paired with many different ingredients. See page 204 for our recipe for these ricotta dumplings and our three favorite ways to serve them.

Ricotta, anchovy & toasted buckwheat

We stole this dish from Septime la Cave in Paris. The freshness of the cheese paired with the saltiness of the anchovy and then the crunch of the buckwheat is a great marriage of flavor and texture. Make this as a snack when you have friends over for a few glasses of something.

SERVES 2
1 cup [250 g] ricotta
4 large or 8 small anchovy fillets
3 tbsp [30 g] buckwheat groats
Extra-virgin olive oil
Juice of ½ lemon
Freshly ground black pepper

Divide the ricotta between two small plates and lay the anchovy fillets over the top. Toast the buckwheat in a dry frying pan over medium heat for 2 minutes, shaking the pan as you go. Scatter over the ricotta.

Dress with a little extra-virgin olive oil, lemon juice, and black pepper and eat with a fork.

Ricotta salata

Ricotta salata has salt added to it and is then aged. It has the creamy taste of ricotta but is much firmer, and because it's been salted it acts as the seasoning in your dish in the same way that Parmesan does (you can use Parmesan as a substitute, although the flavor will be more intense). During the summer months it finds its way into many of our salads, such as the Shaved Fennel, Fava Beans, Peas, Dill & Ricotta Salata (page 53) or with the Chopped Raw Hanger Steak, Pickled Radish & Ricotta Salata (page 95). You can buy it from good cheesemongers and online.

Ricotta on toast with clementine marmalade

You really need the best fresh buffalo ricotta for this breakfast or teatime treat—one that comes wet, still sitting in its milky water. You could replace the clementine marmalade with any homemade jam. You will have plenty of marmalade left over, but an opened jar will keep in the fridge for 2 to 3 weeks.

SERVES 2
For the marmalade
2¼ lb [1 kg] clementines
2½ cups [500 g] superfine sugar
1 tbsp soft dark brown sugar

2 slices sourdough bread
⅓ cup [100 g] fresh ricotta

First make the marmalade. Juice the fruit and then slice the skin and pith into strips. Combine with the juice, cover, and leave to soak overnight in a large pan (this helps to draw out the pectin).

The following day add 4½ cups [1 L] of water to the fruit and juice mixture and simmer over low heat for 1 hour, or until the peel is soft.

Strain the liquid into a clean pan, reserving the peel. There should be about 2 cups [500 ml] of juice remaining; if there is too little, then top it off with water, if too much then return to the stove and keep simmering until reduced. Add the sugar to the liquid, stir over low heat until the sugar has dissolved, then increase the heat and boil hard for about 5 minutes until you reach the setting point of 220°F [105°C] on a candy thermometer.

If you don't have a candy thermometer, you can do the plate test: put a couple of small plates in the freezer for about 15 minutes. Once the jelly has thickened, pour a small amount onto the plate and count to ten. If you can run your finger through the jelly to divide it in two, it means you have jelly. It's a good idea to keep a couple of plates in the freezer in case you need to repeat the test.

Add the reserved peel back to the liquid, making sure the fruit is evenly distributed. Allow to cool and then transfer to sterilized jars and seal.

To serve, toast your sourdough, spread with the ricotta, and spoon on some clementine marmalade.

Tip: The best way to sterilize jars is to wash them on a hot cycle in the dishwasher and then allow to cool. Alternatively you can put them in the oven at 350°F [180°C] for just 5 minutes—any longer and they will end up cracking. And finally you can boil in a large pan for 5 minutes, remove with tongs, and allow to dry naturally.

Pasta

We make a good fresh pasta—fresh is just superior to dried. There is also something very therapeutic and rewarding about rolling out your own homemade pasta, so if you've got a bit of time on a Saturday or Sunday afternoon, then try it.

Fresh pasta

The pasta dough will keep for a couple of days in the fridge, so you can make it in advance—or have some on the weekend with some left over for Monday night's supper.

SERVES 6–8

3¼ cups [400 g] "00" flour
⅔ cup [100 g] semolina flour, plus a little extra for rolling
4 whole eggs
3 or 4 egg yolks
Dash of olive oil

In a large bowl mix both flours together and make a well in the middle. Crack the whole eggs into the well and add the egg yolks.

Break up the eggs a little with a fork and then use your fingertips to start bringing the flour into the eggs in the middle of the bowl. Keep bringing the flour in until a dough starts to form.

Add a splash of olive oil and then turn the dough out onto a lightly floured surface and knead for 8 to 10 minutes, until it is nice and elastic. The dough may seem a little dry at first, but it will soon start to feel smooth and silky. Once your dough is ready, wrap it in plastic wrap and put it in the fridge to rest for a couple of hours.

When you're ready to roll, set up your pasta machine and have a little semolina flour at hand to dust.

Cut the dough into about six manageable pieces. Take one piece and roll it with a rolling pin, just so it is thin enough to fit into the machine. Start rolling it through the machine on the widest setting.

Set your pasta machine on the next setting and put it through again, turning with one hand and catching the dough with the other. After you've rolled it through twice, fold one end of the pasta two-thirds over onto itself and then fold the other third on top. Give it another quick roll with your rolling pin so it will fit through the machine and then roll again, starting at the widest setting. Keep rolling, working your way through the settings so that the pasta becomes thinner and thinner. We usually stop one setting before the narrowest setting. Cut as desired.

Mayonnaise

We use quite a few different types of mayonnaise in our cooking, from traditional aïoli to saffron mayo and harissa mayo. It's always worth knowing how to make a basic mayonnaise, as you can add whatever you fancy to it, because it really is just a case of adding the extra ingredient at the end.

Classic mayonnaise

We make our mayonnaise by hand—all you need are a bowl and a whisk. But you can also make this in a food processor; just make sure that the speed is on slow to medium as you add the oil.

MAKES 2½ CUPS [600 G]
6 egg yolks
1 tbsp Dijon mustard
1 tbsp cider vinegar
Good pinch of salt
1 cup [250 ml] olive oil
1 cup [250 ml] extra-virgin olive oil
Juice of ½ lemon
Salt and freshly ground black pepper

Place the egg yolks, mustard, vinegar, and salt into a large bowl. Mix the two oils together in a measuring cup and then, while whisking, start to pour in the oil in a thin, steady stream.

As the mayonnaise starts to thicken, start adding the oil a little faster, whisking all the time. Once all the oil is combined, stir well and finish with the lemon juice. Taste and adjust the seasoning. You should have a lovely thick mayonnaise. Store in the fridge until needed (it will keep for up to 5 days).

Harissa mayo

Adding harissa paste to homemade mayonnaise means you can mellow out the heat. Eat it with fried fish, in a roast chicken sandwich, or any guilty pleasure you use mayo for—it is better than ketchup. At Rawduck we use it as a base for our breakfast bap, which is a sourdough sandwich of bacon, kale, and a fried egg.

2 tsp harissa paste
⅓ cup [100 g] classic mayonnaise

Simply stir the harissa paste into the finished mayonnaise.

Saffron mayo

Adding saffron to mayonnaise gives it a lovely, golden color and that slightly exotic taste. It's delicious with Fritto Misto (page 209).

Pinch of saffron threads
⅓ cup [100 g] classic mayonnaise

Put the saffron threads in a small bowl with a tablespoon of warm water and leave to steep for about 5 minutes. Stir the saffron-infused water, including the threads, into your mayonnaise.

Aïoli

Aïoli is essentially garlicky mayonnaise and is perfect with fish and shellfish.

1 large or 2 small garlic cloves, grated
¾ cup [200 g] classic mayonnaise

Fold the grated garlic into your mayonnaise as soon as it has come together. Store in the fridge in an airtight container for up to 5 days.

Almond aïoli

Roasting almonds in the oven releases their natural oils, giving them a delicious toasted flavor, which adds another dimension, in a similar way to the Greek dip skordalia, which uses walnuts. Almond aïoli is particularly good with roast fish (see Roast Hake, Fennel, Orange & Almond Aïoli, page 223).

1 large or 2 small garlic cloves, grated
¾ cup [200 g] classic mayonnaise
¾ cup [100 g] toasted sliced almonds

Fold the grated garlic into your mayonnaise. Lightly crush the sliced almonds in a mortar and pestle so they're ground but still hold some texture (you're not looking for powder). Stir into the aïoli.

This is a collection of recipes that you can quickly and easily assemble on a plate to create a delicious weeknight supper or lunch. We pair raw, cured, and salted ingredients to create satisfying flavor dimensions.

Shaved Fennel, Fava Beans, Peas, Dill & Ricotta Salata

An easy summer salad packed full of vibrant summery flavors. It's ideal as a supper for two or doubled up and arranged on a large platter for a sharing feast. The anise from the fennel is set off by the sweet peas and fava beans, and the ricotta salata gives the salad a natural seasoning, so all you need to dress it with are olive oil and lemon.

SERVES 2
1 fennel bulb
⅔ cup [100 g] cooked fava beans
⅔ cup [100 g] cooked peas
Handful of watercress
Juice of ½ lemon
Extra-virgin olive oil
6 oz [180 g] ricotta salata, thinly sliced
Small handful of dill fronds, torn
Salt and freshly ground black pepper

Cut the fennel in half lengthwise and then thinly slice the halves using a mandoline or sharp knife.

Put the fennel slices in a bowl with the fava beans, peas, and watercress. Dress with the lemon juice, olive oil, a little salt, and some pepper and toss together.

Drop the salad onto a serving dish, top with the slices of ricotta salata, and scatter the dill over the top. Add a final splash of olive oil and tuck in.

Cured Salmon, Buttermilk, Shaved Radish & Dill

This is a kind of Scandinavian-inspired recipe—the salmon is cured in the same way gravlax is, which does take a bit of time. But it's such a beautiful and delicate dish, so give it a go. You might only do it for a special occasion, but it's lovely to have as part of a feast. We use radishes in different colors, so do seek them out—it makes for a very pretty dish.

SERVES 4

1 recipe cured salmon (see page 327), about 20 oz [600 g]
Juice of 1 lemon
¾ cup [175 ml] buttermilk
12 radishes (use different colors if you can find them)
Small handful of dill fronds, torn
Freshly ground black pepper

First prepare your cured salmon following the instructions on page 327. You will need to do this at least 3 or 4 days in advance.

Skin the salmon and then cut it into slices about the thickness of a matchstick. Gently lay the salmon slices over four plates so it has a little wave to it.

Add the lemon juice to the buttermilk with a few twists of black pepper and spoon over the salmon.

Thinly slice the radishes using a mandoline and scatter them over the top with the dill. Grind a bit more pepper on top and serve immediately.

Chopped Raw Hanger Steak & Toasted Sourdough

Julian put this dish on the menu when we first opened. It's steak tartare that we subtly fragrance with garlic and rosemary by rubbing the board with garlic and rosemary before chopping the meat, which is how they do it in Italy. This way the meat gently picks up the flavors rather than being overpowered by them.

We use hanger steak, a cut known for its intense flavor. It "hangs" in the diaphragm area and butchers would often keep it for themselves, as it's one of the tastiest bits. It's also the most tender and needs little cooking but is very good eaten raw, which is why it's ideal for this dish. If you can't get hanger, then bavette or flank will work. This is really best served as a starter for a small group and eaten immediately because you don't want to leave it sitting around for too long.

SERVES 2

1 garlic clove
8 rosemary sprigs, leaves picked
5 oz [160 g] hanger or bavette steak, trimmed of excess fat and membrane
1 tbsp capers, chopped
1 shallot, preferably banana shallot, finely chopped
8 cornichons, finely chopped
Juice of ½ lemon
Few dashes of green Tabasco sauce
Extra-virgin olive oil
Sea salt and freshly ground black pepper
Toasted sourdough slices, to serve

First peel the garlic and cut it in half lengthwise. Rub the cut sides of both halves over your cutting board and then discard. Chop the rosemary leaves on the same board, and then rub them over the board. Discard the chopped rosemary.

Place the steak on your now infused board and start dicing. Don't chop the meat too finely; you want it to keep some texture rather than be minced.

Add the capers, shallot, cornichons, lemon juice, and a few dashes of Tabasco to the meat on the board and gently chop everything together, scraping the board with your knife to get the garlic and rosemary flavor into the meat.

Season with salt and pepper and add a little glug of extra-virgin olive oil. Taste and adjust the seasoning; if you like it spicier, add more Tabasco.

To serve, tear your toasted sourdough in half and arrange both halves on the plate. Spoon your chopped hanger over it, ensuring that a little of the toast remains exposed. Finish with a pinch more sea salt and a dash of extra-virgin olive oil.

Salt Cod, Tomato & Olive Oil

You'll find the recipe for salt cod in the Preserving chapter at the back of the book. It needs to be made at least a day in advance but will keep in the fridge for up to 5 days, and there are a couple of recipes in the book that use salt cod, so it's worth salting your own.

We had this during an olive harvest trip with one of our suppliers, George Bennell. He took us to a restaurant in Ileda called Tofal, two hours outside of Barcelona. It's not much to look at, but the food was so simple and very good. The idea is that the owner brings you whatever he wants to bring you (you can, of course, order if you wish to). There are no prices and no menu. At the end he tells you what he wants you to pay. I've been told the bill all depends on what sort of week he is having. A good week: you get a cheap bill. Not so good: well, those prawns will cost you.

One of the dishes we had there was this salt cod, paired with the sweet tomatoes and plenty of early-harvest olive oil.

SERVES 4
1 recipe salt cod, about 14 oz [400 g] (see page 322)
1 lb [500 g] large ripe tomatoes (we love Pink Oxheart tomatoes)
1 small garlic clove, very finely chopped
1 tsp thyme leaves
1 tbsp good-quality red wine vinegar (we use Merlot vinegar)
⅓ cup [75 ml] extra-virgin olive oil
Salt

First prepare your salt cod following the instructions on page 322. You will need to do this at least 10 hours in advance.

To prepare the dish, first skin the tomatoes. Bring a large pan of water to a boil—it should be large enough to hold all the tomatoes. Using a sharp knife, score a little cross at the base of the tomatoes and cut out the "eye" of the tomato at the other end. Have a large bowl of ice water ready, and once your water is boiling, submerge the tomatoes for 15 seconds, then immediately plunge them into the ice water. You'll be able to peel off their skins almost immediately. Halve the tomatoes and remove the cores. →

Tip the tomatoes into a food processer and pulse for 2 minutes, until the tomato pieces are still fairly chunky; don't overblend or you'll end up with a sauce. Add the garlic to the tomatoes with the thyme and vinegar and give it one last pulse. Season with a pinch of salt, but not too much, as you're pairing this with the salt cod.

To serve, use a sharp knife to cut into your cod across the surface area, making wafer-thin slices around 2½ in [6 to 7 cm] long. It's important to get your slices as thin as you can so the flavor remains delicate. Think of how you might buy wafer-thin smoked salmon. Gently lay each of your slices onto four plates but not in a straight line or flat—allow the slices to have a little wave to them. Spoon the tomato pulp over them, covering about a third of the cod, then pour a good glug of olive oil over each plate.

Shaved Zucchini, Pecorino, Lemon & Capers

These beautiful zucchini ribbons look so light and elegant on the plate that all they need are some shavings of pecorino and a few sharp capers dotted around.

We get lots of weird and wonderful zucchini coming through the door in the summer from the Italian markets. They are all quite different in texture and shape, and lend themselves to different styles of cooking. For this dish we usually use "trombetta" zucchini, as they are almost seedless and have a lovely firm texture and curly shape—perfect when you want to serve them raw—although you can use any seasonal zucchini.

This is good on its own as a salad but also goes well with grilled meats.

SERVES 2
2 medium zucchini
2 oz [50 g] pecorino
1 tbsp capers
Juice of 1 lemon
Extra-virgin olive oil
Salt and freshly ground black pepper

Using a vegetable peeler, peel the zucchini from top to bottom into long ribbons. Place the ribbons in a large bowl.

Shave the pecorino into the bowl, add the capers, squeeze in the lemon juice, and add a good glug of olive oil. Mix gently to combine.

Season with salt and pepper, mix one last time, then drop onto two plates.

Black Figs, Labneh, Pistachio & Sumac

It's important to hold out for the best figs and eat them when they're at their peak in late August or September. "Don't accept cheap imitations" is Tom's mantra. And he's right, because when you have the best you don't need to mess—a ripe fig with its sweet, jammy center is a thing of greatness. This dish with pistachios, salty labneh, and the citrus hit of sumac instantly transports you to the sunshine and blue skies of the Middle East.

By the time August comes around we're impatiently waiting for figs because they are one of our favorite ingredients: what's not to love about their amazing, jammy flesh concealed beyond the green or almost whitewashed purple skins?

If your figs are still a little tart, you could add a dash of honey, but when they're fully ripe there is no need. This dish is something to share as a starter or snack or can be part of a casual feast.

SERVES 2
3 tbsp shelled pistachios
⅔ cup [160 g] labneh (see page 323)
4 black figs
1 tsp sumac
Extra-virgin olive oil

Warm the pistachios in a dry frying pan over medium heat; you don't want to color them, just wake them up a little. Lightly crush them and set aside.

Spoon the labneh onto the plates and then, with the back of a spoon, roughly spread it over the plate, keeping some depth and texture (you don't want a flat, even circle).

Tear open the figs and gently place the halves over the labneh. Sprinkle the pistachios and sumac over them and finish by dressing with a little olive oil.

Smoked Cod's Roe, Spring Onion, Marjoram & Olive Oil

Beirut is where we first tried cod's roe and marjoram, a dish that is now one of our Ducksoup classics. The restaurant was recommended to me by photographer Jason Lowe, and he talked of many dishes, including this one. Just like Jason it was bold and ballsy: huge slabs of cod's roe scattered with sliced spring onions and large leaves of very potent aromatic marjoram, which cut through the salty roe. It was quite an acquired taste, but it was something that Julian, who I was traveling with at the time, pared down to put on the menu when we first opened. The dish has come some way since I first had it; we serve it with finely chopped spring onions, lemon juice, and just a small scattering of young marjoram leaves. The flavors in this dish take me right back to the streets of Beirut and that restaurant, with its dilapidated walls swollen with bougainvillea, the air heavy with blossom.

This would be ideal as a summer starter; you don't need much, but it's a really good dish.

SERVES 2
6 oz [180 g] soft smoked cod's roe
1 spring onion, trimmed
Few fresh marjoram or oregano leaves
Juice of ½ lemon
Extra-virgin olive oil
Grilled flatbread, to serve

Gently peel away and discard the outer membrane surrounding the cod's roe.

Place the roe into a bowl and give it a little mash just to loosen it up. Arrange on a serving plate.

Thinly slice the spring onion into rounds and scatter them over the cod's roe, followed by the marjoram or oregano leaves.

Squeeze the lemon juice over the top and then add a good glug of extra-virgin olive oil. Serve with the grilled flatbread.

Mozzarella, Prosciutto, Peas & Dandelion Leaves

There are so many ingredients that work well with mozzarella, and you will find it on our menu throughout the year, paired with different seasonal ingredients. This salad is inspired by that great British summer treat of eating raw, sweet peas straight from the pod. Dandelion leaves are easily foraged—just make sure you give them a good wash. Adding mozzarella and prosciutto turns this into a more substantial lunch or makes it a good accompaniment to lamb chops sizzling on the grill. Serve on large platters and enjoy in the sunshine with a glass of good natural wine. It also works as a quick supper dish—so simple and satisfying.

The buffalo mozzarella that we get from the Ham & Cheese Company in London is so good that sometimes it doesn't even make it back in one piece.

SERVES 2
2 mozzarella balls, about 5 oz [150 g] each
2 oz [60 g] sliced prosciutto
1 lb [500 g] fresh peas in the pod
3 cups [100 g] dandelion greens or arugula leaves
Extra-virgin olive oil
Juice of ½ lemon
Salt and freshly ground black pepper

Tear each mozzarella ball into two halves and place on two plates. Weave the slices of prosciutto on and around the mozzarella.

Shell two-thirds of the peas and scatter them over the plate. Leave the remaining third unshelled; instead just open them up to reveal the peas, still in their pods, and place them around the other ingredients on the plates.

Scatter the dandelion greens or arugula leaves around the dish and just lightly lift everything together to loosen the ingredients and "relax" the dish.

Dress with lots of olive oil and lemon juice and season with salt and pepper.

Salt Cod, Blood Orange, Fennel & Chile

SERVES 2–3
½ recipe salt cod, about 7 oz [200 g] (see page 322)
2 blood oranges
1 small fennel bulb
1 large red chile, seeded and cut into thin strips
Juice of 1 lemon
Extra-virgin olive oil
Sea salt

First prepare your salt cod, following the instructions on page 322. You will need to do this at least 10 hours in advance, although once salted, the cod will keep in the fridge for up to 5 days.

Peel the blood oranges by slicing off the top and bottom and then carefully running a knife around the orange from top to bottom, following the shape of the fruit. Remove all the skin and white pith. Slice the oranges horizontally into ¼-in [5-mm] slices so you see the full shape of the segments in each slice. Place in a bowl.

Remove the fronds from the fennel and tear them into the bowl. (If the fennel doesn't have any fronds, use a few sprigs of dill instead.) Trim off the top of the fennel bulb and then use a mandoline to thinly shave the fennel into the bowl until you get to the root. Add the chile strips. Squeeze in the lemon juice and then dress with olive oil. Use your hands to mix everything together, applying a little pressure or a scrunch here and there to help relax and break up the oranges slightly, allowing the flavors to meld together.

Use a sharp knife to cut into your cod across the surface area, making wafer-thin slices around 2½ in [6 to 7 cm] long. It's important to get your slices as thin as you can so that the flavor remains delicate. Think of how you might buy wafer-thin smoked salmon. Gently lay each of your slices onto your plates but not in a straight line or flat—allow the slices to have a little wave to them.

Using your hands, gently take a handful of your salad and carefully drop it over the cod. Make sure you don't cover the cod completely, as you want to be able to see the fish underneath. Dress with a little more extra-virgin olive oil and a pinch of sea salt.

Prosciutto, Walnuts & Honey

This dish is all about the perfect balance of flavors. The cured meat in this dish is balanced with the sweet honey, while the crushed walnuts add a little texture. We gently toast the walnuts to bring out their natural oils—be careful not to overdo them because they can all too easily burn, making the oil too bitter. The same goes for the honey: don't overdo it or the sweetness will be too overpowering.

We use schiena (see page 115) in this dish because it has a good amount of salty fat on it, but if you can't get schiena then a good fatty prosciutto will also do.

If you like to offer charcuterie at home when friends come over, then give this recipe a go, as it makes things more interesting. It is ideal as a quick a starter dish.

SERVES 2
5 oz [150 g] thinly sliced prosciutto (or schiena if you can find it)
⅔ cup [75 g] lightly toasted walnuts
1 tsp clear honey, preferably unpasteurized (raw)

Gently lay the prosciutto onto the plates. You don't need to be too neat about this: just let the meat fall where it wants to go, but aim for some height rather than flat slices.

Crush the walnuts in your hand and sprinkle them over your prosciutto, then drizzle the honey over the top. And that's it! (You don't need to dress with olive oil, as you have enough fat from the prosciutto.)

Flat White Peach, Goat's Curd & Purple Basil

This is sunshine on a plate! As long as you use the best ingredients you'll immediately find yourself transported to summer sunshine—this is a dish that requires perfectly ripe peaches.

If you buy enough peaches, you can tear a load into a jug and fill it up with ice-cold white wine to give you a lovely refreshing summer drink—a good accompaniment to a day spent pickling and preserving.

Serve this dish with some crusty bread to mop up all the juices—you could even have a plate of prosciutto alongside to help it on its way. If you can't find purple basil (which has a more interesting flavor), try regular basil.

SERVES 2

4 white peaches (we use the flat variety, also known as Saturn or Donut peaches)
Juice of ½ lemon
Extra-virgin olive oil
½ cup [120 g] goat's curd (see page 317)
8 to 10 basil leaves
Salt and freshly ground black pepper

Over a bowl, so you catch all the juices, tear the peaches in half and remove the pits, then roughly tear each half in two (or leave some whole if you want). Drop them into the bowl, add lemon juice, olive oil, and a little pinch of salt, and toss everything together.

Let the peaches fall out of the bowl onto two plates, along with all the dressing. Add a spoonful of goat's curd to each plate. Tear the basil leaves and scatter them over the salads.

Finish with a few grinds of black pepper and a last dash of olive oil.

Radicchio, Blood Orange, Ricotta Salata & Pistachios

This salad pairs their citrus sweetness with the slightly bitter flavor of radicchio, which is also in season at this time of year (you can use any type of radicchio, but we like pink radicchio because it's so pretty). The ricotta salata adds another layer of texture to the dish but also acts as the seasoning.

Blood oranges are the ingredient we all look forward to after harsh winter months; their bright red and orange flesh bursts through those gray winter clouds, offering a little sunshine.

SERVES 2

2 heads radicchio
2 blood oranges
3 oz [75 g] ricotta salata
Juice of ½ lemon
Extra-virgin olive oil
Salt and freshly ground black pepper
Few dill fronds
3 tbsp shelled pistachios, toasted and lightly crushed

Trim the roots from the radicchio, gently pull the leaves apart, and place them in a mixing bowl.

Peel the oranges by first slicing off the top and bottom and then carefully running a knife around the orange from top to bottom, following the shape of the fruit. Make sure you remove all the skin and white pith. Slice the oranges horizontally into ¼-in [5-mm] slices so you see the full shape of the segments in each slice. Add to the bowl.

Cut the ricotta into small nuggets and drop them into the bowl. Dress everything with the lemon juice, olive oil, and a little salt and pepper to taste. Remember, the ricotta is your natural seasoning, so be sure to taste before adding too much salt.

To serve, tip the bowl over a plate and gently coax the salad onto the plates, allowing it to fall naturally. Scatter with a few dill fronds and the pistachios and finish with a drizzle of olive oil.

Roast Artichokes, Prosciutto & Marjoram

For the ancient Greeks and Romans, sweet marjoram was a symbol of love and happiness. If you can grow marjoram, then do so, because as a fresh herb it's really interesting to use; it's a member of the mint and oregano family, with similar notes to oregano, only sweeter and gentler. It's widely used in both Italian and Middle Eastern cooking. Use either marjoram or oregano here, but use the fresh herb, not dried.

SERVES 2
4 long-stem artichokes
Few black peppercorns
2 fresh bay leaves
3 oz [80 g] sliced prosciutto
Few fresh marjoram or oregano leaves
Juice of ½ lemon, plus extra for squeezing
Extra-virgin olive oil
Salt and freshly ground black pepper

Bring a pan of salted water to a boil.

To prepare the artichokes, remove about eight of the outer leaves, or until you get to the paler green inner leaves. Cut the stem of the artichoke about 3 in [8 cm] from the base of the bulb, then using a small knife or vegetable peeler, peel off the outer layer of the stem from the base to the cut end, removing the stringy part of the stem. Slice about ¾ in [2 cm] off the top of the artichoke.

Cook the artichokes in the salted boiling water with a few black peppercorns, a squeeze of lemon, and a couple of fresh bay leaves for 6 minutes, then drain them and allow to cool.

Once the artichokes are cool enough to handle, cut them in half lengthwise and season with salt and pepper. Heat a little olive oil in a frying pan over medium heat and fry the artichoke halves until they are golden brown on each side.

Arrange them on two plates or one serving platter and lay the prosciutto slices in and around them. Scatter the marjoram or oregano leaves over the top and dress with the lemon juice and extra-virgin olive oil.

On Presentation
Tom Hill

Presentation is really important to us at the restaurant. Our aim is to make everything we serve look effortlessly beautiful. As much as we're about making ingredients taste more like themselves, we're also about making them *look* more like themselves. We respect the shapes and forms of an ingredient much in the same way as an architect might a building.

When you're starting with good ingredients we believe you should do as little to them as possible, and plate them in a way that is interesting and beautiful. This means serving them in the right vessel—consider what shape and color will best offset your ingredients—but it also means preparing them in the right way.

We don't have rules as such, as we like things to be unstructured. But if we have one rule, it is just that: don't force it, let it be loose, let it be natural, and let it breathe.

We always tear fruits like peaches or figs—there is something more primal about doing this rather than slicing them with a knife. You are also creating a better surface area for the dressing to cling to; just remember when you tear your fruit to do so over a mixing bowl so that no juice is lost.

When we can, we just smash nuts and leave them in their shells. For example, walnuts: we crush them and leave them in the shell to serve with cheese. It's a beautiful thing to see the nuts in their natural form, shells and all.

We almost always tear herbs. It's never good to cut them so small that they no longer resemble themselves. Herbs can bring so much to a dish, so we want to make their impact as apparent as possible, not only in terms of flavor but also visually. Torn herbs also add more texture to the dish. The same goes for all our leaves—we tear different salad leaves from the root, letting the leaves show off their natural shape.

Mixing salads—to toss or not to toss? Many will say toss, toss, and toss again, but a salad only needs a few light turns before being turned out onto a plate. We prepare salad in a bowl and very gently fold the ingredients once or twice with our fingertips to let air into it. Then we let all the ingredients fall naturally onto the plate. As soon as you start fiddling and placing things, your salad begins to lose its oomph and becomes flat. Have confidence that the ingredients will naturally find their place on the plate and will drop into their own space.

Don't underestimate the glimpse of empty space on your plate. The dish feels more elegant if you leave up to a third of white space on the plate. In the same way, don't feel your ingredients must always go in the center of the plate.

When it comes to cutting and slicing, different rules can be applied to different ingredients. It is useful to think about the ingredient in question: is it fragile and delicate or robust and powerful? For example, we like to cut our kohlrabi wafer-thin, as it gives it a lovely movement and suits its delicacy. Thin slices of kohlrabi seem literally to float to their positions on a plate. Conversely, when we cut hanger steak for steak tartare, we don't chop it so small that it turns into mince; we keep it chunky enough that the meat retains a good texture, which both echoes and aids its big flavor.

Many of our dishes are "deconstructed" so you can see the components. This is a really inviting way to present ingredients, because it means you engage more with what you are eating and see how the elements work together as a whole. For example, our cheesecake is literally triple-fat cheese, fruit, and a crushed digestive biscuit and hazelnut crumb, with each ingredient inhabiting its own space on the plate.

Presentation can run beyond your plates and how you arrange the food on them; a few extras around what you serve can all add to the experience, such as a glass that feels right for the wine you're drinking. We're not into strict rules about which glass to serve with which wine—just simple glasses with short stems or even without stems. We even like our sparkling wines served this way—because sparkling shouldn't only be enjoyed on special occasions. A bit of fizz is full of energy, and is a great way to wash your day away and get you in the right mood. We call this our "little livener"—served in an unpretentious glass with no ceremony needed. The same goes for cocktails—the right glass creates so much excitement, so we're always looking out for glasses with the perfect glass-to-mouth feel. It all adds up to complete everyone's enjoyment.

Good presentation doesn't have to be over-complicated and fussy; just think carefully about the dishes you are serving and let the ingredients speak for themselves.

Taramasalata, Cucumber & Nigella Seeds

Taramasalata is a Greek dish made from tarama—cured and salted cod's roe. It's blended with breadcrumbs and olive oil and is often eaten with raw vegetables or bread. We serve it with cucumber ribbons, as we don't think you need any more bread and it really should be a light appetizer. The cucumber falls beautifully over the tarama, which is finished with a sprinkling of nigella seeds. The result is light, the delicious salty roe contrasting with the cool cucumber.

SERVES 4

1 lb [500 g] smoked cod's roe
1 garlic clove, finely chopped
1 cup [40 g] crustless sourdough bread, broken into pieces
2¼ cups [500 ml] olive oil
Juice of ½ lemon
1 small cucumber
1 tbsp nigella seeds
Extra-virgin olive oil

To make the taramasalata, break up the cod's roe into small pieces, including the skin, and put it into a food processer. Add the garlic and bread pieces and ½ cup [100 ml] water. Blend for 1 minute on medium speed.

Start to add the oil, with the motor still running, in a steady stream until the tarama thickens. If it seems too thick, add a little more water—you are looking for a creamy consistency like mayonnaise. Finish with the lemon juice.

Spoon the taramasalata onto a serving dish and then use a mandoline or vegetable peeler to thinly slice the cucumber along its length into ribbons. Gently place them on top of the taramasalata, allowing them to fall naturally to create a wavy cucumber mountain.

Warm the nigella seeds in a dry frying pan for 2 minutes and then lightly crush them with a mortar and pestle. Sprinkle the nigella seeds on top and dress with a little bit of extra-virgin olive oil.

Mozzarella, Black Figs, Prosciutto & Hazelnuts

The dish is just an assembly of great ingredients, taking seconds to prepare. Make sure the mozzarella is buffalo and is at room temperature; otherwise, the flavor gets lost. We use guanciale (see page 114) but a good, fatty prosciutto will do just as well. Serve this as a quick lunch or starter or, of course, as part of a sharing feast.

This dish came about after I had something similar at an Italian restaurant. The figs were so perfectly in season and the mozzarella so ripe that all it needed were a couple of basil leaves and a drop of balsamic vinegar. We've eliminated a few elements and added our own, so the dish is different from how I first enjoyed it. But at the heart of the dish are the figs and mozzarella, and if these are perfect you can add or eliminate what you like. I dedicate this dish to my friend Sue, who owns land in Gloucestershire where we sometimes forage and cook. One year we found a couple of fig trees with the ripest and sweetest figs, and I made her this dish. She fell in love with it and has been searching for those figs ever since. So Sue, this is for you when you find those figs.

SERVES 2

2 mozzarella balls, about 5 oz [150 g] each
4 black figs
1½ oz [40 g] sliced prosciutto (we use guanciale)
½ cup [50 g] whole toasted hazelnuts, lightly crushed
Extra-virgin olive oil
Juice of ½ lemon
Salt and freshly ground black pepper

Preheat your broiler to high. Tear the mozzarella into two halves and arrange them on your plates. Tear open your figs and place them around the mozzarella, then season with a little salt and pepper.

Lay the prosciutto over your mozzarella and figs and scatter the hazelnuts over all.

Place under the broiler for 5 seconds, just to melt the prosciutto. Dress with olive oil and the lemon juice and serve immediately.

Shaved Squash, Feta, Cumin & Mint

Every year when squash comes into season in early autumn we always think about doing something with them in their raw state, rather than roasting them—much like we do with zucchini. This salad came together from a chunk of squash that Tom kept back from being roasted, and it ended up being one of our favorite raw salads. The delicious, lovely, sweet squash flavor really shines through, and the salty feta comes into its own with the fresh mint and toasted crunchy cumin seeds.

This makes for a very happy plate of food—for lunch, for dinner, or as part of a sharing feast.

SERVES 2
One 7-oz [200-g] piece butternut or other autumn squash, peeled
Juice of ½ lemon
Extra-virgin olive oil
1 tbsp toasted cumin seeds, lightly crushed
3 oz [100 g] feta cheese
Handful of mint leaves, torn
Salt and freshly ground black pepper

First peel the squash (this can be tricky, so use a sharp vegetable peeler). Using a mandoline, thinly slice the squash to create ribbons. You don't want them too thick; otherwise, the salad falls flat and they can be a bit too crunchy.

Put the squash ribbons into a large bowl and dress with the lemon juice, olive oil, cumin seeds, and a little salt.

Tip the salad onto a plate and crumble the feta over it. Scatter the mint leaves on top and finish with a little more olive oil and some black pepper.

Smoked Duck, Black Figs, Ricotta & Hazelnuts

This is one of those assembly dishes: very simple to make but, as with most our cooking, it does rely on getting some decent ingredients. If you can buy a good ricotta rather than just one from the basic range, then it's worth spending that little bit more. Make sure it's fig season because figs don't really taste of much out of season. If you can't get smoked duck from your local deli, a good prosciutto will work here too.

This is a satisfying salad, and is ideal as a weeknight main course or casual weekend lunch.

SERVES 2
4 black figs
Small bunch of watercress
6 oz [160 g] sliced smoked duck breast
½ cup [120 g] ricotta
½ cup [60 g] toasted whole hazelnuts
Juice of ½ lemon
Extra-virgin olive oil
Salt and freshly ground black pepper

Tear the figs in half and place them on two plates, then scatter a few watercress leaves over them.

Lay your smoked duck breast slices over the plates and add a little more watercress.

Spoon the ricotta onto the plates, slightly off center, and then scatter the hazelnuts over all. Dress with the lemon juice and olive oil and season with salt and pepper.

Chopped Raw Hanger Steak, Pickled Radish & Ricotta Salata

We use a lot of pickles in our food, and in the Preserving chapter at the back of the book we explain how to make them. Give yourself a treat one weekend: put aside a Sunday and get pickling. You'll find it very rewarding, and you'll end up with loads of treats to use over the months ahead.

This is a really interesting dish, so do try it and don't be put off by the fact that the steak is raw. This cut lends itself to being eaten this way. Hanger steak is a cut known for its intense flavor; it's also the most tender and needs little cooking to avoid toughness.

After a trip to Japan last year, we came away with lots of ideas for using pickles and ferments in our cooking, and this was something that came out of that. The cheese acts as another layer of seasoning in the dish, while the pickles work well with the raw hanger steak.

SERVES 2
1 recipe pickled watermelon radish (see page 315)
6 oz [180 g] hanger or bavette steak, trimmed of excess fat and membrane
Juice of ½ lemon
Extra-virgin olive oil
¾ oz [20 g] ricotta salata
Salt and freshly ground black pepper

Prepare the pickled watermelon radish, following the instructions on page 315. You will need to do this at least 3 hours in advance.

Using a sharp knife, chop your steak into ¼-in [5-mm] pieces and place them in a bowl. Season with salt and pepper, and add a squeeze of lemon juice and a dash of extra-virgin olive oil. Taste and adjust the seasoning.

Divide the chopped steak between two plates and gently scatter your pickled watermelon radish over it. Grate the ricotta salata on top and finish with a splash of extra-virgin olive oil and some more black pepper.

The recipes you'll find here are fairly quick but need the introduction of heat to kick their flavors into gear. It is a long chapter, as this is how we eat, week in and week out.

From the Stove

Mozzarella, Borlotti & Wild Garlic Green Sauce

Once cooked, borlotti beans, also known as cranberry beans, have a lovely creamy texture and a sweetness to them, which means that they can be enjoyed very simply: a generous serving of a good olive oil and a little seasoning will do nicely. I was introduced to an interesting way of cooking beans by Lori de Mori of Towpath Café, which is in a beautiful spot along London's Regent's Canal. She is also coauthor of the great cookbook *Beaneaters and Bread Soup*. Tuscans are often referred to as "beaneaters" by other Italians because they eat so many beans. After baking their bread they place a glass jar full of beans in the embers along with olive oil, garlic, and sage and leave it to cook slowly overnight. In the morning they have freshly cooked beans—it's called *fagioli al fiasco*, or beans in a flask. Lori gave me one of these flasks as a gift, and we made *fagioli al fiasco* to sit on the bar. Here we've paired the beans with a ripe mozzarella and wild green sauce, which gives it a lovely summer lift.

SERVES 2

One 9-oz [250 g] can good-quality organic borlotti beans in salt
Handful of wild garlic, parsley, and mint, coarsely chopped
    (if you can't get hold of wild garlic, use basil)
6 anchovy fillets, coarsely chopped
Zest of 1 lemon
1 tbsp capers
1 tsp Dijon mustard
1 garlic clove, grated
Extra-virgin olive oil
2 mozzarella balls, about 5 oz [150 g] each
Salt and freshly ground black pepper

Open the beans, pour them into a pan with their liquid, and warm them up. Put the chopped herbs, anchovies, lemon zest, capers, mustard, and garlic into a large bowl with enough extra-virgin olive oil to bind everything together. Stir the green sauce into the beans and warm through on low heat for 1 minute, then divide between two bowls. Tear open the mozzarella balls and place over the beans. Dress with a little more olive oil and some salt and pepper.

Squid & Padrón Peppers

This is a dish that Rory and I had in Copenhagen in a restaurant called Pluto. It had an enormous wall of natural wines. We drank an Aligoté called Love and Pif, and ate pan-fried squid and Padrón peppers. The oil had been infused with the peppers, so it had a bright Padrón-green hue to it—simple, delicious flavors.

SERVES 4
2 lb [1 kg] Padrón peppers
1¼ cups [300 ml] extra-virgin olive oil
4 medium squid, cleaned and prepared (ask your fishmonger)
2 lemons
Sea salt

Start by making your Padrón oil. Cut the tops off half the Padrón peppers and place in a blender or food processor with 1 cup [250 ml] of the olive oil. Blend until smooth. Transfer to a large pan and warm over medium heat for 8 minutes, then set aside to cool. Pass through a fine-mesh sieve, but don't force the oil: let it drip through naturally. This may take around half an hour.

While the oil is dripping, cut open the body of the squid so you have a flat rectangle, and then cut it into three pieces at a slight angle.

Heat a large frying pan until smoking hot. Brush the squid pieces with the remaining ¼ cup [50 ml] oil and season with salt. Fry the squid pieces in batches, along with the tentacles, for 2 minutes on each side. You may need to turn the heat down a little; otherwise, the squid will burn instead of turning golden brown. Set aside. In the same pan, blister the remaining Padrón peppers over medium-high heat, adding a good pinch of salt. Once they've blistered, return the squid to the pan to reheat.

To serve, arrange the different squid pieces and peppers on a large warmed serving platter. Pour the Padrón oil over them and squeeze the juice of 1 of the lemons over all. Quarter the other lemon and tuck it in among the squid and peppers. Finish with a sprinkle of salt.

Lamb Chops, Cumin & Garlic Yogurt

This is a simple dish—the addition of cumin gives the chops a lifting aromatic spice, and the garlic dipping yogurt makes it a perfect feast dish and ideal for barbecues. Alternatively, just squeeze a lemon over it and season with salt, or pour over a little green sauce (see page 35). Cook the chops, pile them up, and spoon your chosen accompaniment over them.

We cook a lot with lamb and buy from Daphne, a supplier in Wales whose lamb is by far the best we've come across. Thank you, Daphne, for such delicious lamb.

SERVES 6
Extra-virgin olive oil
18 lamb loin chops, about 5 oz [150 g] each
¼ cup [25 g] cumin seeds, toasted in a dry frying pan and lightly crushed
3 lemons, cut into wedges
Sea salt and freshly ground black pepper
Garlic yogurt or green sauce (see pages 37 and 35), to serve (optional)

Heat a heavy-bottomed pan or grill pan until smoking hot.

Oil the chops and season with salt and pepper, being sure to really rub it into the chops.

Start by cooking the chops on the fatty rind first: you can do this by holding each chop between a pair of tongs, fat-side down. After 2 minutes and when the fat is browned, lay the chops flat in the pan and cook for 2 minutes on each side, or until nice and brown. Remove from the heat, place on a large platter, and cover with foil. Leave to rest for 5 to 8 minutes, during which time the meat will relax and the juices will flow.

Divide the chops among six plates or bring to the table on the platter, sprinkle the cumin seeds over them, and scatter the lemon wedges in and over the chops. Pour a good drizzle of olive oil over the chops and sprinkle with crushed sea salt. Serve with a bowl of garlic yogurt or green sauce on the side.

Razor Clams, Wild Garlic & Lemon

It's funny how many people seem squeamish about razor clams—
I often think it's because they've got little ET-shaped heads. But if
you've not eaten them, give them a try; their flesh is a little like squid.
A little seasoning here and there and a squeeze of lemon are all you
really need. Ask your local fishmonger for razor clams, although any
other shellfish, such as clams or cockles, would work well with the
wild garlic. If you can't get hold of wild garlic, you can use regular
garlic and torn flat-leaf parsley.

SERVES 2

2 lb [1 kg] razor clams, clams, or cockles
6 tbsp [100 ml] extra-virgin olive oil
Good handful of wild garlic leaves (or 1 large garlic clove,
    thinly sliced, and a handful of torn flat-leaf parsley)
1 lemon, halved
Sourdough bread, to serve

Give the razor clams (or other shellfish) a good rinse under cold
water, but don't wash for too long or you wash away all the flavors
of the sea.

Place a large, lidded frying pan over medium heat. Once your pan is
hot, add the olive oil, then very carefully add the clams—the water
clinging to the shells will spit as it hits the hot pan. Immediately
cover with the lid, as you don't want any of that steam or flavor to
escape (it's the steam that will open up and cook your clams quickly).

After 2 minutes the shells will have started to open. Remove the lid
and tear in the wild garlic in large pieces that will wilt nicely from
the heat. If you are using regular garlic, simply add the sliced garlic
and torn parsley. Replace the lid and cook for a further minute.

Tip everything out onto a large platter or individual plates, add a
squeeze of lemon, and serve with hunks of sourdough to soak up
all those delicious juices.

Blistered Tomatoes, Ricotta & Marjoram

What to do with a million and one tomatoes? In August at the height of summer we see every color, shape, and taste you can imagine— large ones, small ones, tall ones, yellow ones, green ones, rainbow ones. Tomatoes are like little pockets of joy that summer has been keeping for us. The combinations of shapes, sizes, and juices lend themselves to different experiences in this dish, so it's far from just a plate of tomatoes. It's a heavenly tomato salad, great as a starter dish or ideal as part of a few sharing plates.

Don't worry if you can't find the tomatoes we've suggested here— just mix it up a little and use a variety of different ones.

SERVES 4

4 San Marzano or medium red tomatoes
Extra-virgin olive oil
1 garlic clove
1 or 2 thyme sprigs, leaves picked
14 oz [400 g] mixed red and yellow cherry or baby pear tomatoes
2 large Pink Oxheart tomatoes
¾ cup [200 g] ricotta
Handful of fresh marjoram or oregano
Salt and freshly ground black pepper

Preheat the oven to 325°F [160°C]. Cut the San Marzano tomatoes in half from top to bottom and arrange on a roasting pan, skin-side down. Drizzle with a little olive oil.

Thinly slice the garlic clove using a sharp knife or mandoline (be sure to use the guard, as it's when slicing small ingredients like this that you can cut yourself). Lay the garlic slices over the tomatoes, sprinkle the thyme leaves over them, and season with salt and pepper. Roast for 45 minutes to 1 hour, or until the tomatoes are nicely caramelized.

Meanwhile, place a frying pan over high heat and add a little olive oil. When the pan starts smoking, add the small red cherry tomatoes and blister them so that the skin goes black and starts to pop. Season with salt, place on a pan to cool, and set to one side. →

Slice the yellow cherry tomatoes in half but cut them at a slight angle rather than straight across—this will give them a bit more shape and adds to the texture of the dish. Set aside. Cut the large Oxheart tomatoes in half from top to bottom and then cut each half into 3 or 4 chunks, alternating the angle of your cut.

Once your roasted tomatoes have started to cool, you're ready to serve. Divide the roasted tomatoes among four plates. Place the large chunks of tomato in and around the roasted tomatoes, then add a small pile of blistered red cherry tomatoes, and finally scatter the yellow tomatoes over them. Add a spoonful of ricotta (slightly to the side rather than dead center) and sprinkle with fresh marjoram or oregano leaves. Finish with a drizzle of extra-virgin olive oil and season with salt and pepper.

Asparagus & Bottarga/Berkswell

There are many things to do with asparagus, and early in the season we like to keep it simple and serve it with just olive oil, salt, and lemon so that you can really taste the flavor the earth has worked so hard to produce. But as we move through the season we spruce things up: a grating of bottarga, a cured fish roe that works as a natural seasoning, falling into the umami category as cured foods so often do; or adding Berkswell cheese (see page 115), which is a classic that Mark Hix used to serve—it has a good balance of saltiness and creaminess so it works very nicely.

SERVES 4
Extra-virgin olive oil
16 fat asparagus spears, woody ends snapped off
2 oz [60 g] bottarga or Berkswell (depending on which
    dish you are making)
Juice of 1 lemon
Salt and freshly ground black pepper

Heat a large, heavy-bottomed pan or grill pan until smoking. While the pan is heating up, rub the asparagus with olive oil and season with salt and pepper.

Add the asparagus spears to the pan and cook for 2 minutes on each side (you'll need to do this in batches). You want them to have a nice charred look, but don't cook for too long or they will go soft.

When the spears are all cooked, scatter them onto plates, letting them fall naturally rather than being arranged side by side. They can overlap and do whatever they feel comfortable doing.

Using a Microplane or the finest side of your grater, grate either the bottarga or Berkswell over the asparagus. Squeeze the juice of your lemon over the top, and add a couple of grinds of black pepper. Finish with a drizzle of extra-virgin olive oil and serve.

On Charcuterie & Cheese
Tom Hill

We use many different types of cured meats in our cooking, each with its own unique characteristic. Sometimes the difference is only slight, but it's enough for us to make a decision to pair it with a specific ingredient. Our supplier is the Ham & Cheese Company in London. They've been sourcing directly from suppliers in Italy and France since 2007.

We use a fair bit of cheese on our menu, too, and always pair it thoughtfully with other ingredients, whether salad leaves, vegetables, or meat. You can now buy a wide variety of different cheeses online, and as many of them keep well, it's worth getting a small selection.

For the recipes in this book, where we have used something a little more out of the ordinary (particularly when it comes to charcuterie), we have suggested an alternative.

Charcuterie

Capocollo It's cured neck of pork seasoned with wine, rolled in dried herbs, and aged for 4 months. There's lots of lovely fat running through the meat.

Culatello/Culaccia Culatello is one of Italy's most expensive cured pork cuts. It is a single muscle cut from the hind leg. It's then aged in ancient caves where it gets a natural mold, which gives it a wonderful flavor. Culaccia is a brand of culatello that is aged in the mountain air of the Parma Apennines.

Finocchiona This coarse-ground pork meat salami is seasoned with wild fennel pollen. It is our favorite salami for cutting into nuggets to enjoy with a glass of chilled red wine.

Guanciale The guanciale we use is made from the Nero Calabrese pigs, famed for their great cheeks (*guancia* is the Italian word for "cheek"). They are rubbed with pepper and then aged for 8 to 10 months.

Lonza affumicata This is young loin of pork that is salt cured for just 2 weeks before being lightly smoked. The flavor is gentle and it's very lean—ideal for those who don't like too much fat.

Malenca Malenca is a wet version of bresaola, with an almost pickled flavor. Ours is made by a former lawyer in Lombardy, who sits it in a bath of salt, pepper, cinnamon, nutmeg, cloves, bay, and garlic for a week before lightly smoking it.

Schiena This is a thick layer of pork back fat cured with some of the loin still attached; it is then lightly smoked. It is a good introduction for people who are a little unsure of lardo.

Cheese

Berkswell This is a really delicious English sheep's milk cheese from the West Midlands. It has a sweet, nutty flavor, not unlike manchego. As a young cheese it is creamy, but when aged for five months or so, it gets firmer and more crumbly—this is when we think it's at its best.

Gorgonzola dolce This is a beautiful creamy cheese from Lombardy, with a sweet and slightly nutty flavor. This is very well balanced with the mineral-like flavor of the blue mold that runs through the cheese. It is best enjoyed after it has sat out of the fridge for an hour or so.

Goat's curd Curd is getting more and more popular, which also means it's easier to find. It comes from the first part of the cheese-making process, when the curds are separated from the whey. It's creamy and moist but still has some of those sharp characteristics of a goat's cheese.

Pecorino Such a great cheese, available in lots of different "ages." It's a sheep's milk cheese that is made all over Italy, although Sardinia is known for its pecorino. A young pecorino will be smooth, not too firm, and quite mild in flavor. The longer it is aged, the more salty and crumbly it becomes. It works well with sweet flavors, and we often pair it with pears, honey, and hazelnuts.

Ricotta The fresh ricotta we use is Sairass Fresca, which is a sheep's milk cheese from Piedmont. It's wrapped in a muslin sack and has the most beautiful creamy texture with a slight nutty flavor to it. Unlike other ricottas, which tend to be a little grainy, this is lovely and smooth.

Ricotta salata This great little cheese, called *cacioricotta* in Italy, is like Parmesan in that it can be used to season a dish. Although it retains some of the creaminess of fresh ricotta, it has been drained and aged, so it is quite firm and—as the name suggests—salty. We finely grate it or just cut it into shavings for salads and pasta.

Squid, Olive Oil, Chile & Basil

We usually cook squid quickly with intense heat, but here everything goes in cold and gently warms up together, cooking the squid much more slowly and creating a completely different texture. Although not Asian in its flavors, this dish was inspired by a trip to Japan made by Tom, Rory, and myself. Tom was fascinated by how they prepared their squid when serving it raw, scoring it so carefully that it became soft with a melt-in-the-mouth texture. Here, Tom has experimented by cooking the squid in a different way. When people come into the restaurant and order this, they always order another straight after. You can ask your fishmonger to prepare your squid.

This is a good starter or as a sharing plate with 3 or 4 other dishes.

SERVES 2

2 medium squid, each about 12 oz [350 g], cleaned and prepared
⅔ cup [150 ml] extra-virgin olive oil
2 tsp dried chile flakes
Juice of 1 lemon
Handful of basil leaves
Sea salt
Good sourdough bread, to serve

To open the squid out flat, first remove the tentacles and set aside. Insert a knife into the body and cut along one side. Clean away any membrane left inside and open out the body into a rectangle.

Using a very sharp knife, cut the squid into strips as thin as you can. This will take a bit of time but is well worth it because it makes the squid much more tender. Cut the tentacles into single pieces and mix with the rest of the squid.

Put the squid, olive oil, and chile flakes in a large, heavy-bottomed frying pan over low heat. Stir gently as the pan warms up; the chile flakes will start to infuse the oil and the squid will turn white. Keep stirring, and when all the squid has turned milky white and feels firm, add the lemon juice, tear in the basil leaves, and add a good pinch of sea salt. Serve with chunky-cut sourdough bread to mop up that delicious infused oil—you don't want any going to waste.

Pan-roasted Pears, Speck, Gorgonzola & Walnuts

The combination of flavors and textures in this dish makes it the perfect winter salad. When the pears are at their best, the creamy Gorgonzola and salty speck provide as much satisfaction as any hearty winter dish. Enjoy it as a lunch or dinner when you need a bit of sustenance but don't want anything too heavy.

We use Comice pears when they are in season: they are deliciously sweet and hold their shape and texture when cooked. For best results we cook them on the stove in a heavy-bottomed frying pan; this way you can ensure an even color without overcooking them.

SERVES 2
2 pears
Extra-virgin olive oil
5 oz [150 g] thinly sliced speck
3 oz [100 g] Gorgonzola
⅔ cup [75 g] lightly toasted walnuts
Salt and freshly ground black pepper

Cut the pears into quarters and remove the seeds from the cores.

Warm a little olive oil in a heavy-bottomed frying pan over medium heat and add the pears, cut-side down. Cook until golden brown, about 2 minutes, then turn and brown the other side.

Arrange the pears evenly on the plates. Gently place and curl the speck in and around your pears, then, using a teaspoon, add nuggets of Gorgonzola over the pears and the speck. Crush the walnuts in your hand and scatter them over the top. Dress with a little olive oil and season with salt and pepper.

Angel Hair Pasta, Sage, Rosemary & Parmesan

This is simplicity at its best: minimal ingredients but the best you can find, meaning a good extra-virgin olive oil and a decent Parmesan cheese—all it needs then is the addition of a few fresh herbs. You could serve this at a casual lunch or even for dinner and everyone would be impressed because it's just so straightforward and satisfying. Less is more, as they say.

SERVES 2

6 oz [160 g] angel hair pasta
⅔ cup [150 ml extra-virgin olive oil
8 large sage leaves, coarsely chopped
Few rosemary sprigs, leaves coarsely chopped
1 oz [20 g] Parmesan
Salt and freshly ground black pepper

Bring a large pan of water to a boil; once it starts to boil, add a generous pinch of salt, then add the pasta and cook for 3 minutes.

Meanwhile, place a frying pan over medium-low heat and add the olive oil. Add the sage and rosemary to the pan and gently cook the herbs for about 2 minutes, long enough to infuse the oil and soften the herbs. Watch the pan, because you don't want to let them burn or go crisp.

Drain the cooked pasta, keeping a little of your pasta water. Add the pasta to the frying pan and use a pair of tongs to toss it around your pan for about 1 minute, coating it in the oil. Add a couple of tablespoons of the reserved pasta water to help spread your infused oil through the pasta.

Remove from the heat and grate in about half the Parmesan. To incorporate it into the pasta, use tongs to pull mounds of the pasta up toward you.

Season with a little salt and pepper and divide between two plates. Finish by grating over the remaining Parmesan, along with a couple of grinds of black pepper.

Pan-roasted Carrots, Goat's Milk Yogurt & Za'atar

During the summer months, when French sand carrots, or *carottes de sable*, are in season, we like to do this dish because the cute little carrots look so irresistible and have a sweet flavor. Normal carrots will work just as well, although they will be less sweet, so if you've got mounds of carrots in your vegetable drawer and don't know what to do with them, this is a fine way to put them to good use.

This is a good dish to have with roast meat or fish, or simply as part of a vegetarian feast if you're doing a few plates to share.

SERVES 4

2 lb [1 kg] finger carrots
Extra-virgin olive oil
2 tbsp sesame seeds
1 tbsp sumac
1 tbsp dried wild oregano
1 cup [250 g] goat's milk yogurt
Juice of ½ lemon
Salt

Scrub the carrots to remove any dirt, but don't peel them. Remove any green ends or leaves. If you're using larger carrots, cut them into ¼-in [5-cm] wedges on an angle (rather than straight across) to give a bit of visual texture to the dish.

Heat a frying pan over medium-high heat, add a glug of olive oil, and fry the carrots with a good pinch of salt until they are nicely colored on all sides, 5 to 6 minutes. You should be able to cook the carrots completely like this, but if they are still quite firm you can finish them off in the oven. Test them with the point of a sharp knife—they should still be a little firm.

To make your za'atar, toast the sesame seeds in a dry frying pan and combine with the sumac, oregano, and a pinch of salt. Set aside.

To serve, scatter the carrots over a large serving plate, spoon the goat's milk yogurt over them, and then generously scatter over the za'atar. Finish with a drizzle of olive oil and the lemon juice.

Grilled Shrimp, Lemon, Salt & Chile

You hardly need a recipe to make this dish, but we've put it into the book because it's nice to be reminded of the simple things in life. You can do these on the grill instead of in a frying pan. The idea is that you cook the shrimp in the prepared salt, but carry on dipping as you eat, peeling the shrimp as you go, dipping and generally getting covered in all the delicious juice and salt.

We use wild shrimp, so do get these if you can; otherwise just buy the best that you can.

SERVES 4
Zest of 2 lemons
1 tbsp sea salt
1 tbsp dried chile flakes
24 large raw shell-on shrimp
Olive oil
Lemon wedges, to serve

First prepare your salt by grinding together the lemon zest, salt, and chile flakes in a mortar and pestle. Set to one side.

Place a heavy-bottomed pan or grill pan over medium-high heat until smoking hot. Oil the shrimp and season with some of the chile salt, then grill for 3 minutes on each side.

Serve on a platter with lemon wedges and a spoonful of the delicious zesty salt on everyone's plate.

Charred Fennel, Peas, Prosciutto & Pecorino

This dish, with its lively flavors of summer, combines the charred sweetness of fennel, the crunch of a sweet fresh pea, and the saltiness of the prosciutto and pecorino—perfect with a glass of white wine. You can easily create this at home and enjoy it at a table in the sun.

SERVES 2
1 large fennel bulb, with fronds
Extra-virgin olive oil
14 oz [400 g] fresh peas in the pod
Juice of ½ lemon
3 oz [80 g] sliced prosciutto
1 oz [40 g] pecorino
Few dill fronds, torn
Salt and freshly ground black pepper

Pick off the fronds from the fennel and set to one side. Cut the fennel in half from top to bottom, then lay the cut-side on the board and cut each half in half lengthwise again, leaving the quarters joined at the root so the fennel holds together.

Place a heavy-bottomed frying pan over high heat while you brush the fennel with oil and season with salt and pepper. When the pan is smoking, cook the fennel on all sides until slightly softened. This should take about 4 minutes on each cut-side. You want your fennel to still have a good bite to it; you don't want it completely soft.

While the fennel is cooking, bring a large pan of salted water to a bowl and have a bowl of ice water to hand. Shell the peas and blanch for 1 minute, then refresh in the cold water. Drain and tip them into a bowl. Once your fennel is cooked, allow it to cool slightly and then mix it in with the peas. Tear over the fennel fronds (reserving a few to finish the dish) and add the lemon juice and some olive oil.

Drop the fennel and peas onto your serving plate and give it a gentle shake so that the fennel moves around the plate naturally. Lay the prosciutto slices over the top, and then use a small knife or peeler to cut nuggets of pecorino to scatter over it. Finish with salt and pepper, more olive oil, and a sprinkling of fennel and dill fronds.

Asparagus, Peas, Nasturtium Leaves & a Soft-boiled Egg

Eggs are one of Tom's favorite ingredients—if he can put an egg with something, he will. And I don't blame him, but like all our ingredients it's about the quality of the egg. Sadly, a bad egg won't add much to your dish. We use free-range eggs because they have beautiful rich yellow yolks. It's worth upgrading, as it will make all the difference when you break through the white and see that sunshine yolk smiling back at you. Nasturtium leaves have a unique, almost pepper-like flavor and are really easy to grow in a pot or back garden.

SERVES 4

4 eggs
8 fat asparagus spears, woody ends snapped off
1 lb [500 g] small peas in the pod
2 cups [40 g] nasturtium leaves, picked and washed (or use arugula)
2 cups [40 g] chervil leaves or chives
1 lemon
Extra-virgin olive oil
Salt and freshly ground black pepper

Start by cooking the eggs. Bring a pan of water to a boil and get a bowl of ice water ready. Add the eggs to the boiling water and cook for 5½ minutes (set a timer). As soon as they are done, drop them into the ice water to stop them from cooking further. Meanwhile, bring another pan of well-salted water to a boil and cook the asparagus for 2 to 3 minutes, or until the stalks are just tender. You can test this by removing a spear with your tongs and giving the stalk a gentle squeeze. Once ready, drain and plunge immediately into ice water.

Once the eggs are cool enough to handle, peel and set to one side. Shell the peas and set these aside too. When the asparagus is cool, drain well and cut each spear into thirds, but rather than cut straight across, angle your knife so that you expose more surface area of the cut asparagus. Scatter the asparagus over a large serving dish and sprinkle the peas, nasturtium leaves, and chervil (or arugula and chives) over them. Grate over the zest of about half the lemon. Slice the eggs in half lengthwise and place them in and around the salad. To serve, dress with extra-virgin olive oil and a squeeze of half the lemon, and season with salt and pepper.

Wild Mushrooms, Egg Yolk & Parmesan

If you live near any woods, then you should try to forage your own mushrooms—it's an enjoyable way to get out into the open. The most common one you'll find is the chanterelle. These grow en masse and are easy to check against your mushroom guidebook. The season is usually March to April and then September to November. If you get lucky it's very rewarding to hurry back home and put your mushrooms straight in the pan. Alternatively, your greengrocer should stock a variety in season.

SERVES 4

1¾ lb [800 g] mixed wild mushrooms, such as chanterelles or hedgehog
6 tbsp [100 ml] olive oil
2 large garlic cloves, very thinly sliced
¾ cup [200 ml] chicken stock
3 tbsp butter
Handful of flat-leaf parsley, coarsely chopped
Juice of 1 lemon
4 free-range egg yolks
1½ oz [40 g] Parmesan
Salt and freshly ground black pepper
Toasted sourdough bread, to serve

Pick through the mushrooms to make sure there are no twigs or leaves, and give them a little brush to remove any soil. Tear any larger mushrooms in half.

Place a large frying pan over high heat and add the olive oil and garlic. Cook for about 30 seconds, or until the garlic just starts to color, then add the mushrooms. Cook until the mushrooms have released their water and started to fry, 5 to 8 minutes. Once the mushrooms start to fry and take on some color, pour in your chicken stock and cook for 5 minutes, until the stock has reduced by two-thirds. Stir in the butter and parsley and cook for a further 2 minutes. Season the mushrooms with salt and pepper and squeeze in a little lemon juice.

Divide the mushrooms among four plates. Gently tip a yolk into the center of the mushrooms and add a generous grating of Parmesan and more pepper. Serve with toasted sourdough.

Bresaola, Ricotta & Chanterelles

In this dish we use Malenca (see page 114), which is cured in a similar way to bresaola but with aromatics, so it has a slightly different flavor to it, which makes it more interesting. You can use bresaola, but try not to buy it presliced. This recipe was inspired by a dish that Tom, Pete, and Orlaith (two of our managers) had when visiting Valli Unite, one of our favorite wine suppliers in Italy. The dish was originally made with bresaola, truffle, and ricotta and is another example of how simple things can be when you're using good ingredients. Try this as a sharing platter or as a small feast with one other dish. The ingredients and flavors just say autumn in the Italian countryside.

SERVES 2
2 tbsp extra-virgin olive oil, plus extra for drizzling
5½ oz [160 g] chanterelles or other wild mushrooms, wiped with a dry cloth
6½ oz [180 g] bresaola or Malenca (if you come across it)
⅔ cup [160 g] ricotta
Juice of ½ lemon
Salt and freshly ground black pepper

Heat the extra-virgin olive oil in a large frying pan over medium heat and fry the mushrooms for 5 to 8 minutes, or until they have released their water and they start to crisp up a little. Season well with salt and pepper and set aside to cool.

Place your bresaola or Malenca on the plates; don't lay it flat—give it some body and a wave so that it has movement. Spoon the ricotta onto the plates, covering about a third of the plate, and then add the mushrooms, slightly overlapping your ricotta.

Season with salt and pepper, squeeze over the lemon juice, and add a drizzle of olive oil.

Charred Eggplants, Garlic Yogurt, Toasted Cumin Seeds & Mint

Eggplant is always one of our biggest-selling vegetarian dishes; whichever way we prepare it, it sells, and this dish in particular. This is easily cooked for a quick weeknight dinner or as part of a vegetarian sharing feast.

SERVES 4

8 baby or 4 medium eggplants
Extra-virgin olive oil
¾ cup [200 g] Greek yogurt
1 garlic clove, very finely chopped
Juice of ½ lemon
2 tablespooons cumin seeds, toasted and lightly crushed
Few pinches of dried chile flakes
Handful of mint leaves
Salt and freshly ground black pepper

Place a heavy-bottomed pan or grill pan over high heat until smoking hot. Meanwhile, cut the eggplants in half lengthwise and rub with olive oil, salt, and pepper.

Once the pan is nice and hot, place the eggplants cut-side down in the pan and cook for 3 minutes. Turn and cook the skin side for another 3 minutes. (Cook for a few minutes longer if using medium eggplants.) The eggplants should be cooked but still have a little firmness to them, and will have taken on a lovely smoky flavor. Once they're cooked, arrange them cut-side up on a large serving platter and set aside.

Mix together the Greek yogurt, garlic, lemon juice, and a drizzle of olive oil. Season with a pinch of salt.

Spoon the yogurt over and around the eggplants and then sprinkle over the cumin seeds and chile flakes. Tear over the mint leaves and drizzle with a little more olive oil.

Braised Onions, Goat's Curd, Mint & Sourdough

We owe this dish to Raef Hodgson of 40 Maltby Street, originally just called Raef's place, but everyone who loved natural wine knew about it. People would start early—it has that great atmosphere which doesn't make you feel bad for wanting a glass of wine at 11 a.m. on a Saturday. We buy a lot of our wines from Raef and his partner, Harry. Raef's brother Kit cooked a dish similar to this in those early days: little bits of toast topped with curd, onion, and mint. Our version is more brothlike, but this is where the inspiration came from. Thank you, 40 Maltby Street.

SERVES 2
Extra-virgin olive oil
10 oz [300 g] sweet red onions (we like new-season tropea) or small shallots, preferably banana shallots, unpeeled, with ends trimmed and roots intact
2 garlic cloves, unpeeled
Few thyme sprigs
6 tbsp [100 ml] white wine
1 cup [250 ml] chicken stock
3 tbsp [40 g] butter
2 slices of sourdough bread
3 tbsp goat's curd (see page 317) or very good unpasteurized cottage cheese
Few mint leaves
Salt and freshly ground black pepper

Place a lidded medium pan over medium heat, add a glug of olive oil, and then add your whole unpeeled onions or shallots and garlic cloves. Roast in the pan until the skins start to go golden brown, then add the thyme and white wine and allow to bubble for 1 minute.

Pour in the chicken stock, season with salt and pepper, and put on the lid. Cook for 8 to 10 minutes, or until you can easily pierce the onions with the point of a knife. Remove the lid, add the butter, and cook for a further 2 minutes. While the onions are cooking, toast the sourdough, either under a hot broiler, in a toaster, or in a grill pan.

To serve, place a slice of toasted sourdough on each plate and divide the onions between them. Spoon a dollop of curd onto a third of the plate, pour a little onion juice over it, and tear over the mint leaves.

Zucchini, Fava Beans, Peas,
Tahini Yogurt, Pomegranate & Dill

This is a classic Ducksoup dish; it appears on our menu at some point every summer. We start to serve it as soon as all those bright green vegetables start coming into season. We char the zucchini, which helps to give more depth of flavor. It's a beautiful array of different greens, and the pink pomegranate seeds scattered on at the end make it even prettier. This is a good warm salad, vegetarian main course, or accompaniment to simple grilled or roasted meats.

SERVES 4

1½ lb [800 g] zucchini
Extra-virgin olive oil
1 lb [500 g] peas in the pod
1 lb [500 g] fava beans in the pod
1 pomegranate
Juice of 1 lemon
1 cup [250 g] tahini yogurt (see page 37)
Handful of dill fronds
Salt and freshly ground black pepper

Cut each zucchini into thirds on the diagonal; if you do this on alternate angles you will get a more interesting shape, which helps add texture to your dish.

Place a large frying pan over medium-high heat until hot. Add a couple of tablespoons of olive oil and add your zucchini, frying them until they are golden brown on all sides. Season with salt as you go. Once cooked, remove from the pan and set to one side.

Bring a large pan of well-salted water to a boil while you shell the peas and fava beans. Once shelled, add to the water and blanch for just 1 minute and drain. Plunge straight into a bowl of ice water to stop them from cooking further.

Remove the seeds from the pomegranate by cutting it in half and then holding it over a bowl, cut-side down on your spread palm. Hit the back of the pomegranate with a wooden spoon or rolling pin so that the seeds drop out into the bowl. If you have trouble, try turning the half inside out and gently coaxing the remaining seeds out with your fingers. →

Drain the peas and fava beans well and add to a bowl with the zucchini. Dress with the lemon juice and some olive oil and season with salt and pepper.

It's now time to assemble your ingredients. Spoon the tahini yogurt into the middle of a large plate and then use the back of your spoon to gently spread it out. Don't go for a thin, even circle—you want some texture. Spoon your vegetables over the yogurt, making sure that you don't cover it completely—you want them to sort of look like they're bobbing in a tahini pond. Tear over your dill, being sure to keep the fronds intact, and finally spoon the pomegranate seeds over the dish—you want to try to spoon little groups into any gaps, rather than just having a sprinkling of single seeds here and there. Finish with a bit more lemon juice and a good helping of olive oil.

Sweetbreads, Peas, Pancetta & Chanterelles

We like offal at Ducksoup, and sweetbreads are probably one of the most popular types we put on the menu. This is one of those dishes where all the ingredients really work together. It's a good dish to do as a starter or quick supper if you're a fan of sweetbreads. If you can't get hold of chanterelles, then something like oyster mushrooms will work here.

SERVES 2
7 oz [200 g] lamb sweetbreads
2 tbsp cider vinegar
1 lb [500 g] fresh peas in the pod
Olive oil
4-oz [120-g] piece of pancetta, cut into lardons
3 oz [80 g] chanterelles or oyster mushrooms
1 cup [250 ml] lamb stock
¼ cup [50 g] butter
Few mint leaves
Juice of ½ lemon
Salt and freshly ground black pepper

Bring a pan of salted water to a boil, one that is large enough to hold all the sweetbreads. Meanwhile, prepare the sweetbreads by running them under a cold tap until the water runs clear.

Once the sweetbreads are clean, add them to the pan along with the cider vinegar and gently simmer for 5 minutes, or until they start to firm up. Once cooked, drain and allow to cool. When they're cool enough to handle, remove the outer membrane and any white gristle.

Shell the peas and set to one side. Heat a large frying pan over medium heat and add a glug of olive oil. Season the sweetbreads with salt and pepper and fry on one side until golden brown, about 2 minutes. When they're ready to turn, add the pancetta and chanterelles to the pan, turn the sweetbreads and allow everything to gently cook together for 2 minutes more.

Add the peas and stock and cook everything for a further 5 minutes, or until the peas are cooked and the stock has reduced by half. Stir in the butter and tear in the mint leaves and cook for a further 2 minutes. Season with salt, pepper, and a squeeze of lemon juice and serve.

We love to cook but don't always have the time, though a home warmed with the smell of a cooked meal is one of life's unrivaled pleasures. These recipes will give you the pleasure of cooking without your becoming a slave to the kitchen.

146

Orzo Pasta, Spicy Tomato Sauce & Feta

The Italians use orzo in soups and stews, as it's a good way to bulk out a dish without filling yourself up too much. Feta gives this dish an added saltiness, but not in the same way that Parmesan would—it's more gentle. This dish reminds of how good a well-made feta can be. We love this dish as a summer weeknight supper.

SERVES 2

1 lb [500 g] large tomatoes (we love Pink Oxheart tomatoes)
3 tbsp extra-virgin olive oil, plus extra for drizzling
1 tsp cumin seeds
1 tsp nigella seeds
1 small onion, diced
1 garlic clove, crushed
1 tsp dried chile flakes
1 bay leaf
1 tsp paprika
4 oz [120 g] orzo pasta
3½ oz [100 g] feta
Few leaves of fresh oregano

First skin the tomatoes. Bring a large pan of water to a boil. Using a sharp knife, score a little cross at the base of the tomatoes and cut out the "eye" of the tomato at the other end. Have a large bowl of ice water ready, and once your water is boiling submerge the tomatoes for 15 seconds, then immediately plunge them into the ice water. You'll be able to peel off their skins immediately. Set to one side.

In a large frying pan, temper the cumin and nigella seeds in the olive oil over low heat for 1 minute, then add the onion and cook until soft. Add the garlic, chile flakes, bay leaf, and paprika and cook for 2 minutes. Coarsely chop the tomatoes, add to the onions, and simmer for 10 minutes. You're looking for a soupy consistency, so if you need to add a little water, then do so. Season with salt and pepper. While your sauce is cooking, bring a large pan of salted water to a boil and cook your orzo pasta for 10 minutes, or according to the package instructions. Drain and add to the tomato sauce.

Let everything cook together for a couple of minutes. To serve, divide between two bowls, crumble the feta over, and sprinkle with the fresh oregano and a drizzle of olive oil.

Grilled Poussin & Green Sauce

Rory and I had this dish at a restaurant called Isa in Brooklyn, recommended by my friend Eleanor Morgan. It was a sunny autumn Saturday and we sat outside and ate this poussin, which was juicy and sweet, the aromatic zesty herbs giving the dish an additional sunny zing. For us this is one of those perfect alfresco weekend lunches washed down with something white and crisp.

A poussin is a month-old chicken—delicious and sweet in flavor. Because they're small they only take 25 minutes to cook, which makes them ideal for a quick supper. And in the summer they are great on the grill. The green sauce is also great with roast chicken or grilled quail.

SERVES 2

Extra-virgin olive oil
2 whole poussins
1 cup [10 g] parsley leaves
1 cup [10 g] mint leaves
1 cup [10 g] basil leaves
1 oz [25 g] salt-packed anchovies (3 or 4)
1 tbsp capers
½ tsp Dijon mustard
1 tbsp good-quality red wine vinegar
½ lemon, cut into 2 wedges, to serve
Salt and freshly ground black pepper

Preheat the oven to 400°F [200°C]. First spatchcock the poussins. Place a poussin breast-side down on a cutting board and use sharp kitchen scissors to cut down either side of the backbone. Remove the backbone, turn the poussin over, and then push down hard on the breastbone to flatten it out.

Season the birds with salt and pepper and rub with a little olive oil.

Heat a heavy-bottomed pan or grill pan until it's smoking and then place the birds in the pan, skin-side down. Turn over once one side is charred, 5 to 6 minutes, and char the other side. Repeat so that both sides are nicely charred—you may have to do this one at a time, depending on the size of your pan.

Remove from the pan and place the birds in a couple of roasting pans. Roast in the oven for 20 to 25 minutes.

While the birds are in the oven, make the green sauce by coarsely chopping the herbs and anchovies. Place them in a bowl and then combine with the capers, mustard, and vinegar and add a generous helping of extra-virgin olive oil to bind everything together.

Once your birds are ready, serve straight from the oven, spooning over a little of the sauce and letting the rest fall naturally onto the plate. Add a lemon wedge to each plate to finish.

Grilled Quail, Mograbiah & Preserved Lemon

This is a Middle Eastern–inspired way with quail—it came about when Tom started preserving lemons. We kept making more and more jars but hadn't decided what to do with them, and then this came along. Mograbiah is also known as giant couscous (see page 41).

This is nice as part of a feast at any time of year; or after you've enjoyed a few smaller sharing things you can bring a platter of these cute roasted birds sitting on a bed of mograbiah as a main course. You will find the recipe for preserved lemons on page 325.

SERVES 4

4 jumbo quails, each weighing 6 to 7 oz [180 to 200 g], cleaned and heads off
6 tbsp [100 ml] extra-virgin olive oil, plus extra to dress
Pinch of dried chile flakes
1 tbsp paprika
1 onion, finely diced
2 garlic cloves, sliced
2 fresh bay leaves
1 tbsp chopped fresh thyme
1 preserved lemon (see page 325), pulp removed, cut into thin slices
4½ cups [1 L] chicken stock
7 oz [200 g] mograbiah (giant couscous)
Handful of cilantro leaves
Garlic yogurt (see page 37), to serve (optional)
Salt and freshly ground black pepper

First spatchcock the quail. Place a quail breast-side down on a cutting board and use sharp kitchen scissors or poultry shears to cut down either side of the backbone. Remove the backbone, turn the quail over, and then push down hard on the breastbone to flatten it out. Repeat with the remaining quails. Set aside while you prepare the mograbiah.

Warm the oil in a pan over low heat, add the chile flakes and paprika, and temper for 1 minute. Add the onion and cook gently for 5 minutes before adding the garlic, bay leaves, thyme, and preserved lemon. Cook for a further 2 minutes, then pour in the chicken stock and bring to a boil. Add the mograbiah and bring back to a boil, then reduce the heat and simmer for 8 to 10 minutes, stirring occasionally, until the mograbiah is slightly tender, but still with some bite.

While the mograbiah is simmering, start cooking the quail. Heat a grill pan until smoking hot while you rub the quails with oil and then season with salt and pepper. Place them in the pan, skin-side down, and cook for 3 minutes—you will need to turn the heat down slightly; otherwise, they will burn too much. Turn over and cook the other side for 5 minutes. Finally turn them over again (skin-side down) and cook for a further 2 minutes. Transfer to a plate and allow to rest for 5 minutes.

To serve, spoon an equal amount of the mograbiah onto each of four serving plates (or use one large serving platter), pop a quail on top, and tear over the cilantro leaves. Serve with a dollop of garlic yogurt (see page 37), if desired.

Grilled Quail, Labneh, Shaved Kohlrabi, Pomegranate & Dill

An easy dish to prepare, as you're only cooking the quail. Kohlrabi belongs to the cabbage family and is a cross between a radish and a turnip. I first came across them on a trip to Tripoli, but now I see them everywhere—and thank goodness, because they are fresh, clean, and delicious. Here the meat is paired with labneh and is a good example of how you can match labneh with grilled meats. We often think of labneh as the "enabler" because it's the link between the meat and the vegetables, helping to bring all the flavors together.

SERVES 4

4 jumbo quails, each weighing 6 to 7 oz [180 to 200 g], cleaned and heads off
Extra-virgin olive oil
1 pomegranate
1 large kohlrabi
1 tsp dried chile flakes
Juice of 1 lemon, plus extra for squeezing
Few dill fronds
½ cup [120 g] labneh (see page 323)
Salt and freshly ground black pepper

First spatchcock the quail. Place a quail breast-side down on a cutting board and use sharp kitchen scissors or poultry shears to cut down either side of the backbone. Remove the backbone, turn the quail over, and then push down hard on the breastbone to flatten it out. Repeat with the remaining quails.

Heat a grill pan until smoking hot while you rub the quails with oil and then season with salt and pepper. Place them in the pan, skin-side down, and cook for 3 minutes—you will need to turn the heat down slightly; otherwise, they will burn too much. Turn over and cook the other side for 5 minutes. Finally turn them over again (skin-side down) and cook for a further 2 minutes. They should be a little pink. Transfer to a plate and allow to rest for 5 minutes.

Meanwhile, remove the seeds from the pomegranate. Cut the fruit in half and then, over a bowl, place the pomegranate cut-side down on your spread palm and hit the back of it with a wooden spoon or rolling pin; the seeds will drop into the bowl. If you have trouble, try turning the half inside out and gently coaxing out the last few seeds with your fingers. Set to one side.

Using a mandoline, shave the kohlrabi into nice thin ribbons and then place in a bowl. Add the chile flakes, lemon juice, half the dill, and a glug of oil and season with sea salt. Give it a good mix and set to one side.

When you're ready to serve, place a good spoonful of the labneh just off the center of each plate and then, with your hands, give the kohlrabi salad one more mix. Place a little pile of the salad next to the labneh, making sure it doesn't fall flat. Place the quail next to your labneh and salad, scatter the pomegranate seeds and remaining dill fronds over them, and drizzle with a final glug of olive oil, a pinch of salt, and a little squeeze of lemon juice.

Warm Castelluccio Lentils, Purple Sprouting Broccoli & Tahini Yogurt

A wholesome dish for winter. We use Italian Castelluccio lentils here, but you can just as easily use Puy. You can also use normal broccoli instead of the purple sprouting variety. This is one of our vegetarian classics and works as a weeknight supper: simple and satisfying.

SERVES 2

⅔ cup [125 g] Castelluccio or Puy lentils
3 tbsp extra-virgin olive oil, plus extra
½ tbsp cumin seeds
½ tbsp dried chile flakes, plus extra for seasoning
1 onion, diced
2 garlic cloves, finely chopped
2 bay leaves
½ cup [60 g] skin-on whole almonds
1½ cups [375 ml] vegetable stock
14 oz [400 g] purple sprouting broccoli
Handful of mint and flat-leaf parsley leaves
⅓ cup [100 g] tahini yogurt (see page 37)
Salt and freshly ground black pepper

First clean the lentils. Put the lentils in a large pan of unsalted water and bring to a boil. Drain and rinse under cold water and then set aside. In a separate pan, warm the olive oil with the cumin and chile flakes and temper for 2 minutes. Add the onion, garlic, and bay leaves and cook for 5 to 8 minutes, or until the onion is soft but not colored.

Meanwhile, pulse the almonds in a food processor until they are coarsely chopped. Add to the onions and cook for 2 minutes. Add the lentils, pour in the stock, and cook for a further 10 minutes, until the lentils are tender but not too soft.

Meanwhile, cook the broccoli in a pan of boiling salted water for 2 minutes. Drain, refresh under cold water, and set aside. Place a grill pan over high heat while you lightly brush the broccoli with oil. Season with salt and pepper and when the pan starts smoking add the broccoli. Grill for 2 minutes on each side. Once the lentils are cooked, tear in the mint and parsley and season. Divide the lentils between two serving bowls, top with the broccoli, and spoon the tahini yogurt over. Drizzle with olive oil and add a pinch of chile flakes.

Ditalini, Ricotta, Swiss Chard & Lemon

A quite comforting dish, this is sort of like macaroni cheese, but not in the traditional sense, as it uses ditalini, which is a kid's pasta in Italy. The use of ricotta cheese makes this dish fresh and light, with a little zing from the lemon zest.

This is really easy to make. It's great as a quick midweek dinner but equally good as a Saturday lunch with a glass of wine.

SERVES 2
5½ cups [160 g] ditalini pasta
8 oz [250 g] baby Swiss chard or spinach
⅓ cup [100 g] ricotta
Grated zest of 1 lemon
Extra-virgin olive oil
Grated Parmesan, to serve (optional)
Salt and freshly ground black pepper

Bring a large pan of water to a boil. As soon as it's boiling, add a good pinch of salt. It wants to be as salty as the Mediterranean sea, so don't be shy. Drop in your pasta. The pasta should take 10 minutes to cook, so set a timer for 9 minutes, as you'll be cooking the chard in the same water as the pasta (but do check the cooking times on the package if you are using a different type of pasta—you only want the chard to cook for 1 minute).

When your timer pings, add the chard and cook for 1 minute more. Drain the pasta and chard over a bowl, reserving about ¾ cup [200 ml] of the cooking water.

Return the pasta and chard to the pan and place over medium heat. Add the ricotta and give a gentle stir (don't stir too much, as you want to retain little nuggets of cheese in the sauce). Add just enough cooking water to loosen the pasta up and make a creamy sauce.

Season with salt and pepper and then divide between two serving bowls. Finish with the grated lemon zest, a drizzle of olive oil, and a twist of black pepper. Add a little grated Parmesan if you want a stronger flavor.

Summer Zucchini, Orecchiette, Parmesan & Oregano

When zucchini are in season, you will find lots of different types available—and we like to take full advantage of them. For this dish we use the round green and yellow zucchini that you find at most farmers' markets or greengrocers. Of course, it works just as well with the green variety we're more familiar with. Zucchini in season will taste much better than those flown halfway around the world. At this time of year we often just prepare and eat our zucchini raw because you get to taste that subtle, sweet nuttiness.

SERVES 4
2 large yellow zucchini
4 small round green zucchini
6 tbsp [100 ml] extra-virgin olive oil
8 small garlic cloves, thinly sliced
11 oz [320 g] dried orechiette pasta
2⅔ cups [80 g] Parmesan, grated
Handful of fresh oregano
Juice of ½ lemon
Salt and freshly ground black pepper

Preheat the oven to 400°F [200°C] and put a large pan of water on to boil. Place a heavy-bottomed frying pan over medium-high heat.

Prepare the zucchini by cutting the yellow ones into 2-in [5-cm] chunks on the diagonal. Cut the round green zucchini in half lengthwise, then cut each half in half again at an angle. Place all the zucchini in a large bowl with the olive oil. Season with salt and pepper and toss to coat.

Your frying pan will be well and truly hot now. Heat some oil and cook the green zucchini cut-side down until golden brown. Turn and cook the other cut-side again until golden brown. Once cooked, transfer to a roasting pan. Cook the yellow zucchini in the same way, transferring to the roasting pan when they're done. Add a little more olive oil to the frying pan, reduce the heat, and fry the garlic for about 5 minutes, until lightly colored. Add to the zucchini and then place the roasting pan in the oven for around 8 minutes, or until the zucchini are cooked but still have some bite to them.

Once the zucchini are in the oven, you can cook your orecchiette. Throw a big pinch of salt into your pan of boiling water and cook the orecchiette following the instructions on the package. Once cooked, drain the pasta, being sure to reserve some of the pasta water.

Remove the roasting pan from the oven and place on the stove over medium heat. Add the pasta and half the Parmesan and give it a good stir. Pour in just enough of the reserved pasta water to loosen the dish, about ¼ cup [60 ml]. Give the pan a shake, tear the oregano in half and scatter it in, add salt and pepper, and give it a final stir.

You can serve this dish straight from the roasting pan or transfer to a serving platter. Top with the remaining Parmesan, the oregano, and the lemon juice.

Crab, Tomatoes, Agretti & Caper Mayonnaise

Agretti is a green, salty vegetable grown in coastal regions—traditionally it has a short season starting in April, but it is cultivated more and more these days and is gaining popularity, so do ask your greengrocer to source some for you. It's wispy in appearance (like a beard) and is known as monk's beard in the UK. Agretti's saltiness adds natural seasoning to any dish, and here it's paired with crab, but it is delicious just dressed with lemon juice and olive oil or as part of a salad.

SERVES 2

3 oz [100 g] agretti
1 tbsp capers
¼ cup [60 g] mayonnaise (see page 47)
4 medium tomatoes
3 oz [80 g] lump crabmeat
Juice of ½ lemon
Extra-virgin olive oil
Salt and freshly ground black pepper

Bring a large pan of salted water to a boil. Blanch your agretti in the water for 30 seconds and then drain; refresh in cold water and drain again.

Coarsely chop your capers and stir them into the mayonnaise.

Slice the tomatoes into rounds about ¼-in [5-mm] thick and scatter them over two serving plates.

In a large bowl, combine the crabmeat, agretti, lemon juice, and a glug of olive oil and season with salt and pepper. Spoon the mixture over the tomatoes, making sure you don't cover them completely (you want to be able to see the tomatoes and get a sense of the layers of ingredients).

Do the same with the caper mayonnaise, placing a spoonful over another section of the plate. Finish with a drizzle of olive oil and a twist of black pepper.

Turmeric Chickpeas, Kale, Garlic Yogurt & Burnt Lemon

A good example of how, with a little clever spicing and flavor combinations, everyday ingredients become more than the sum of their parts. The humble chickpea is transformed into a comforting and homely dish boosted with a hit of garlic yogurt and caramelized lemon juice. We use El Navarrico giant Castilian chickpeas, which you can buy online. Dried chickpeas will always give you a better result, but if you are short on time you can use canned—just buy the best you can afford.

This is a good dish to throw together on a winter's evening, but it can also be enjoyed as part of a feast.

SERVES 2
3 tbsp olive oil
½ tbsp cumin seeds
½ tbsp nigella seeds
½ tbsp dried chile flakes
1 medium onion, diced
1 tbsp ground turmeric
2 garlic cloves, crushed
9 oz [250 g] good-quality canned chickpeas
1 lemon
9 oz [250 g] kale
2 tbsp garlic yogurt (see page 37)

Warm the olive oil in a large pan over low heat and temper the cumin seeds, nigella seeds, and chile flakes for 2 minutes. Add the onion and cook until soft. Add the turmeric and crushed garlic and cook for a further few minutes.

Add the chickpeas and all the liquid in the can, and cook for 30 minutes over medium heat, or until most of the liquid has evaporated.

Meanwhile, put a large pan of salted water on to boil while you char the lemon. Have a bowl of ice water nearby. Heat a grill pan or frying pan until hot. Cut the lemon in half at a 45-degree angle and place cut-side down in the pan—you want dark charring lines.

Blanch the kale in the boiling salted water for 30 seconds and immediately refresh in the ice water. Squeeze out any water from the kale and arrange loosely on a large plate. Spoon the chickpeas over and top with the garlic yogurt. Arrange the burnt lemons on the side.

Roast Eggplants, Lentils, Soft-boiled Egg, Garlic Yogurt & Dukkah

This all-in-one dish is ideal for a winter filler or as a large one-pot dish if you're having people over—just multiply the quantities if you are cooking for more. The flavors are earthy and spicy and your kitchen will take on the life of an exotic Middle Eastern kitchen as you cook this. The yogurt and mint provide the perfect amount of coolness to the dish. This is one of our best-selling vegetarian dishes and you'll discover why when you eat it.

SERVES 2

1 lb [500 g] large tomatoes (we love Pink Oxheart tomatoes)
2 eggs
⅔ cup [125 g] Puy lentils
3 tbsp extra-virgin olive oil, plus extra for brushing
1 tsp cumin seeds
1 tsp nigella seeds
1 small onion, diced
1 garlic clove, crushed
1 tsp dried chile flakes
1 bay leaf
1 tsp paprika
2 baby eggplant
2 heaping tbsp garlic yogurt (see page 37)
2 heaping tbsp dukkah (see page 39)
Few mint leaves
Salt and freshly ground black pepper

First skin the tomatoes. Bring a large pan of water to a boil—large enough to hold the tomatoes. Using a sharp knife, score a little cross at the base of the tomatoes and cut out the "eye" of the tomato at the other end. Have a large bowl of ice water ready, and once your water is boiling, submerge the tomatoes for 15 seconds, then immediately plunge them into the ice water. You'll be able to peel off their skins almost immediately. Set to one side.

Cook your eggs in the same pan of boiling water for 6 minutes. Once they are cooked, plunge them into the ice water. When they are cool enough to handle, peel and set to one side.

Meanwhile, bring a pan of water to a boil and cook the lentils for 20 minutes. Drain and set aside. →

In a large frying pan over low heat, temper the cumin and nigella seeds in the olive oil for 1 minute, then add the onion and cook until soft, about 5 minutes. Add the garlic, chile flakes, bay leaf, and paprika and cook for 2 minutes.

Coarsely chop the tomatoes and add to the onions. Add the lentils and simmer for 10 minutes. You're looking for a soupy consistency, so if you need to add a little water, then do so. Season with salt and pepper.

While your lentils are simmering away you can blister your eggplant. (If the lentils are ready before the eggplant, remove from the heat and set aside, then warm through when you're ready to serve.) Heat a frying pan over medium-high heat until it's smoking hot. Cut the eggplant in half lengthwise, brush with olive oil, and season with salt and pepper. Place them in the pan, cut-side down, and cook for 2 minutes, or until they start to blister. Turn and cook on the other side for 2 minutes. You may need to turn the heat down when you turn them over, because you don't want the skin to burn and go bitter. Once they are cooked, transfer to a pan to cool.

To serve, divide the lentils between two bowls and place the blistered eggplant halves on top. Spoon the garlic yogurt over the top. Cut the eggs in half and place yolk-side up just on top of the yogurt. Finally, spoon or sprinkle your dukkah on and around the dish and tear over the mint leaves.

Seasonal Greens, Tahini Yogurt, Freekeh & Burnt Lemon

If you want something healthy but filling, then this is the dish. We usually put something like this on the menu in January, when we're all suffering and need a good detox but aren't ready or willing to starve ourselves. We talk about freekeh in our Larder chapter (see page 41); it's one of our preferred grains and is gaining lots of popularity for its high nutritional value. If you can't get freekeh (although you can buy it online), you can replace it with bulgur wheat.

You can use any greens you like, but we prefer to use rapini, as it has pungent flavor and gives the dish a bit of a kick.

SERVES 2
¾ cup [125 g] freekeh or bulgur wheat
1 lemon
14 oz [400 g] rapini, cavolo nero, kale, or purple
    sprouting broccoli (or a mixture)
⅓ cup [100 g] tahini yogurt (see page 37)
Extra-virgin olive oil
Salt and freshly ground black pepper

Place a grill pan over medium-high heat and bring a pan of salted water to a boil.

Bring a second pan of salted water to a boil for the freekeh—you will need twice the volume of water to freekeh. Add the freekeh and cook for 10 to 12 minutes, or until the water has all been absorbed by the freekeh and the grains have doubled in size. Drain any excess water and keep warm in a covered pan.

Meanwhile, cut the lemon in half and place cut-side down in the grill pan for about 5 minutes, or until it is caramelized and burnt. At the same time, cook your greens for 2 minutes in the boiling water. Drain but don't refresh.

To serve, arrange the greens on two plates and divide the freekeh between them, next to the greens. Spoon the tahini yogurt next to the freekeh and place a burnt lemon half, cut-side up, on each plate. Dress generously with olive oil and season with salt and pepper.

Spring Vegetable Fritters, Cucumber Yogurt & Curry Leaves

The finishing touch of curry leaves with these fritters makes for a delicious snack when you have friends over. But be warned: these will disappear fast. We've chosen spring vegetables here because there are so many lovely spring ingredients to celebrate. Frying at home can put some people off, but these are really just shallow fried.

SERVES 4

For the fritters

8 oz [250 g] asparagus, woody ends snapped off, sliced into ¼-in [5-mm] rounds
8 oz [250 g] peas
8 oz [250 g] fava beans
4 spring onions, sliced
1 small bunch wild garlic leaves (replace with 1 crushed garlic clove if wild garlic is not in season)
1 lemon
1 egg
2 cups [250 g] "00" flour
2¼ cups [500 ml] ice-cold sparkling water
Vegetable or sunflower oil, for frying
Handful of curry leaves
Good pinch of sumac
Salt and freshly ground black pepper

For the cucumber yogurt

½ cucumber, cut lengthwise, seeds scooped out
Pinch of salt
2 cups [500 g] Greek yogurt
3 tbsp extra-virgin olive oil
Juice of ½ lemon
1 garlic clove, crushed
Handful of mint leaves, coarsely chopped
Salt and freshly ground black pepper

Start with the cucumber yogurt. Coarsely grate the cucumber into a sieve set over a bowl and rub a good pinch of salt into the cucumber. Set aside for about 45 minutes to allow the cucumber to release its water.

Meanwhile, make the fritter mix. Place the asparagus into a large bowl with the peas, fava beans, spring onions, and wild garlic leaves (or crushed garlic clove). Zest the lemon over the top (keep the lemon to use in the cucumber yogurt) and season with salt and pepper.

In a separate bowl, mix the egg with the flour and then slowly add the sparkling water, whisking constantly. You want the consistency of thick cream, so go easy, as you may not need all the water. Pour this batter mixture over the vegetables and mix well. →

Heat a generous amount of vegetable or sunflower oil in a large, heavy-bottomed pan until a small piece of bread turns golden in 10 seconds.

While the oil is heating, finish the cucumber yogurt by giving the cucumber a gentle squeeze to remove the last bits of water. Then place in a mixing bowl with the yogurt, olive oil, lemon juice, garlic, and mint. Give everything a quick whisk—it should have a bit of texture to it—and season with salt and pepper.

The oil should now be hot enough so, working in batches of four, drop tablespoons of the fritter mix into the pan. (To stop the batter mixture from sticking to your spoon, dip the spoon into the oil first—but make sure the spoon is dry when you do this.) Be careful when dropping the fritters into the oil, as they may splash a little. Fry the fritters for 5 to 6 minutes, or until golden brown, and use a slotted spoon to turn them halfway through the cooking time. Remove with a slotted spoon and transfer to some folded paper towels to drain off some of the oil. Give them a pinch of salt, keep warm, and then do the next batch in the same way.

Once all the fritters are done, drop the curry leaves into the oil; again, be careful as they will crackle and spit as they cook. Fry for 1 minute, remove, and drain on paper towels.

To serve, spoon the cucumber yogurt onto plates. Arrange the fritters and curry leaves on top of the yogurt and sprinkle with the sumac.

Pappa al Pomodoro & Ricotta

A classic Italian dish for using up stale bread; this is our version with the addition of ricotta. This is a good weeknight supper or weekend lunch, or if you've got a few friends over it will do very nicely. Perfect on a hot summer's afternoon.

SERVES 4

⅔ cup [150 ml] extra-virgin olive oil, plus extra to serve
1 onion, diced
2 garlic cloves, chopped
2 lb [1 kg] very ripe large tomatoes (we love Pink Oxheart tomatoes)
2 cups [80 g] stale crustless sourdough bread, torn into bite-sized pieces
1 tsp good-quality red wine vinegar (we use Merlot vinegar)
¾ cup [200 g] ricotta
Salt and freshly ground black pepper

Heat the oil in a pan over very low heat and add the onion. Cook for about 12 minutes; you want the onion to go soft and translucent but not brown. If the pan does start to stick, just add a splash of water. When the onions are soft, add the garlic and cook for a further 2 minutes.

Halve the tomatoes and remove the cores, then cut into chunks. Add to the pan (skin, seeds, and all) and season with salt and pepper. Cook for a further 10 minutes over low heat so the tomatoes break down and release all their juices.

Add the bread to the tomatoes, along with the vinegar. Give it all a good stir and then turn off the heat. Leave it to sit for 30 minutes for the flavors to relax into each other and so that it cools down—this is not a dish to serve hot.

Check the seasoning, as it may need a little more salt or vinegar. Divide among four bowls, and top with a dollop of ricotta and a good glug of extra-virgin olive oil.

Charred Fennel, Mussels, Cockles & Fregola

If you were on a beach, having built a fire with a large pan hoisted over the top, this should be the dish you'd cook. It's so easy. It's just fennel, white wine, shellfish, and all that lovely sea juice soaking up into the fregola, which is a type of pasta from Sardinia, similar in appearance to giant couscous. As well as the juices and flavors of the mussels and cockles, the fregola is given extra depth from the charred fennel, which adds a gentle smoky flavor.

But it's not every day we're on that beach, so instead invest in a large stockpot and cook this on a hot weekend day with a bottle of chilled white wine at the ready. If you have a pan big enough, double this recipe to serve four people.

SERVES 2
1 large or 2 small fennel bulbs
Extra-virgin olive oil
14 oz [400 g] mussels
9 oz [250 g] cockles
4 oz [125 g] fregola
3 tbsp olive oil
2 garlic cloves
1 cup [250 ml] dry white wine
1 lemon
Sea salt

Remove the fronds from the fennel and set to one side. Cut the fennel in half from top to bottom and then lay each half cut-side down on a cutting board. Use a sharp knife to slice through each fennel half, angling your knife to get a more interesting shape, but leave the root intact so that the bulb half keeps its shape.

Heat a grill pan until smoking hot. Brush the fennel with oil and season with salt and pepper, then add to the pan and grill until well colored on all sides. Set to one side.

Rinse the mussels and cockles well under cold water, removing any beards from the mussels by pulling them sharply toward you. Discard any shells that do not close firmly when tapped with the back of a knife.

Bring a pan of salted water to a boil, add the fregola, and cook for 8 to 10 minutes. Drain and return to the pan, then cover and keep warm.

Heat 3 tbsp of olive oil in a large pan over medium heat. Place the garlic cloves on your cutting board, add a pinch of sea salt, and use the flat side of a heavy knife to crush the garlic; add to the pan and fry for 1 minute.

Add the charred fennel, fregola, and shellfish and increase the heat to high. Give the pan a shake and cook everything for a further minute, then add the wine; immediately cover your pan with a lid. You want to retain all the steam, as this will open up the shells. Cook with the lid on for 5 minutes, giving the pan a good shake halfway through so that everything combines. It's important to shake, not stir, as you don't want to remove the lid and lose any of the heat. After 5 minutes, remove the lid to have a little peek and see how the shellfish is doing, and give everything a quick stir. If you think the shells are not open enough, cook for a further 2 minutes.

By this time the shellfish will be ready, so tear in your fennel fronds, squeeze the lemon over, and pour gently out onto a large platter (or divide evenly between plates). Check that all the shells have opened and discard any that remain firmly closed.

On Natural Wine
Rory McCoy

When I first tried natural wine it tasted so real,
so juicy, so full of life. I thought, "I could drink
this stuff for hours," and I did. Natural wine
is now a huge part of life at Ducksoup. These
wines are alive, and taste so much of how
and where they have been grown, without the
use of chemicals to dumb them down.

Natural wines have strong critics and divided
opinion. Of course there are bad natural wines,
just as there are bad conventional wines,
but there is also a world of great natural and
biodynamic wines, and I wouldn't listen to
anyone who writes them off out of hand. Find
out for yourself—France and Italy are both
good places to drink natural wine and find out
about different producers.

If you like well-looked-after ingredients, you
will enjoy the independent character of these
wines and the back stories of how they are
grown. The people producing these wines are
caring and passionate about what they do,
which speaks volumes.

What is natural wine?
The first thing to say about natural wine is that
it's wine. The grapes are handpicked, pressed,
squashed, fermented, and bottled, and the wine

is drunk with or without food. Many people try to pin down exactly what natural wine is. My take is this: it is wine made in a natural way, by adhering to the rules set by nature. There are no man-made chemicals, pesticides, or herbicides used in the growing of the grapes or the wine production. It is wine how wine used to be made.

There are three categories in the changing world of modern-day natural winemaking:

Organic
Organically made wine is a good place to start, but the "organic" label can be misleading. For a wine to be organic, synthetic chemicals cannot be used when growing the grapes, but that doesn't extend to what's added during the winemaking process. So organic winemakers might add preservatives like sulfites (SO_2) or use cultivated yeasts to give their wine a characteristic flavor. Natural winemakers do not add cultivated yeast, so the process happens at its own pace, using the friendly bacteria that already live and breathe close by. Sulfites are chemicals that protect wine from oxidation and bacteria. By adding them, a winemaker can stop and restart the winemaking process at different stages. Here man controls the wine, whereas with natural wine the winemaker follows nature and listens to what the wine wants.

Biodynamic
A movement started by Rudolph Steiner in the 1930s, biodynamic farming is about working as one organism, with everything feeding each other in harmony. It also follows the cycle of the moon, harnessing its power. Its proponents argue that this proactive attempt to bring life to the soil produces a more flavorful grape.

Natural
Natural winemaking eliminates all chemicals. Natural wine tastes different from conventional wine because the acidity levels are higher and the mineral flavors more powerful. Natural wine does not rely on added sulfites in the same way that conventional winemaking does. After the Second World War sulfites were introduced into general farming to help endangered crops. Today they're used in conventional winemaking to produce uniform flavors and consistency. But over time this use of agrochemicals has damaged soil health and has contributed to the buildup of pathogens—another good argument for choosing to drink natural.

Naturally occurring SO_2 can be present in winemaking—the question is if SO_2 is added can they be classified as truly "natural" wine. The next stage of classification is *vin S.A.I.N.S.,* which translates as "without any additives or (added) sulphites." This brand-new, exciting

association of wine producers features
wines that are produced with nothing added,
nothing removed.

On drinking natural wine
It's important to think about the wine you're
drinking. Those added chemicals can give you
a hangover. Fact. But price is also an issue. As
with food, a very cheaply priced wine sends
warning signs about its cost-conscious mass
production. Natural wines, on the other hand,
take more time: the fragility of the work and
environment means the winemaker has to be
present to watch and nurture his crops. Since
this is all done by hand or horse, natural wine
is therefore more expensive.

Natural wine is full of what nature originally
intended. You aren't just omitting chemicals,
you're adding essentials that are lost in today's
diets. You are drinking unfiltered, pure grape
juice, fermented with enzymes, nutrients,
good yeast, and bacteria.

There you are—a glass of wine has never tasted
so good, or been so good for you. *Santé!*

Crab Fettuccine, Tomatoes & Bush Basil

Here we use cherry tomatoes, which are small and so sweet. Get
them on the vine, if possible. The bush basil adds a further hint of
the Mediterranean—it's not quite as powerful as regular basil and
so doesn't overpower the crab. In Greece they have huge pots of
bush basil outside the front doors. The idea is that visitors run their
hands through the leaves before entering, so as to freshen up.

SERVES 2

5 oz [150 g] cherry or pear tomatoes on the vine
2 tbsp extra-virgin olive oil, plus extra for drizzling
1 garlic clove
8 oz [160 g] lump crabmeat
Pinch of dried chile flakes
6 oz [160 g] fresh fettuccine (see page 45), or use dried
Juice of ½ lemon
Few bush basil sprigs (or regular basil), torn
Salt

Bring a large pan of salted water to a boil. Heat a frying pan until
smoking, then add the tomatoes, a drop of the olive oil, and a pinch
of salt. Give the pan a little shake here and there and fry the tomatoes
for about 5 minutes, or until the skins start to blister and burn
slightly. Once amply blistered, pour out onto a plate and set aside.

Gently heat the remaining olive oil in a large pan over medium heat.
Meanwhile, thinly slice the garlic using a mandoline—use the guard—
and add to the pan (or if you prefer you can slice the garlic by hand
but as thinly as possible). As soon as the garlic starts to turn golden
brown, add the tomatoes and all their juices. Give them a quick stir
and then add the crabmeat and chile flakes. Stir together and cook
over low heat for 5 minutes.

While this is cooking, add the fresh pasta to the pan of boiling
water and cook for 2 minutes. (If using dried pasta, follow the
instructions on the package.) Drain the pasta, reserving a couple
of tablespoons of the pasta water, and add the pasta to the tomato
and crab sauce, with a little of the reserved pasta water.

Season with salt (you don't need pepper because of the chile flakes). Use tongs to pull mounds of the pasta up toward you so that you thoroughly coat the pasta with the sauce. Squeeze in the lemon juice and divide between two plates.

To serve, sprinkle the basil leaves over the pasta and drizzle with olive oil.

Cavolo Nero & Pappardelle

Cavolo nero (or Tuscan kale) is our favorite of all the cabbages—we love its dark, pillow-like leaves. Its perfect, green mouthful of goodness works in so many different ways, and you can always rely on it to add a rich, dark green color to your dishes. For this recipe, rather than making the traditional pesto, we experimented with cavolo leaves, which is less potent than using basil. Ellie Hix, who worked with us for a while, swears by this recipe when she wants to impress. Add it to your repertoire if you're looking to do the same.

SERVES 2

2 garlic cloves
18 oz [500 g] cavolo nero
Zest of 1 lemon
⅔ cup [80 g] pine nuts, toasted
1⅓ cups [40 g] Parmesan, grated
3 tbsp extra-virgin olive oil, plus extra for drizzling
6 oz [160 g] fresh pappardelle (see page 45), or use dried
Salt and freshly ground black pepper

Bring a large pan of generously salted water to a boil. Once boiling, add the garlic cloves, then reduce the heat and simmer for 8 minutes.

Meanwhile, trim the woody stalks from the cavolo nero, leaving you with just the soft outer leaves. (You can keep the stalks for pickling; see page 313.) Remove the garlic from the pan with a slotted spoon and place in a food processor. Put the cavolo nero leaves in the pan and cook for 8 minutes. Remove with a slotted spoon and add to the garlic in the food processor, along with a couple of tablespoons of the cooking water. Blitz until you have a smooth purée.

Add the lemon zest, half the pine nuts, and half the Parmesan and season with salt and pepper. Process again, while slowly pouring in the olive oil in a steady stream through the feed tube. Don't overwork the purée; otherwise, it will start to go gray. Once the sauce is ready, drop your fresh pasta into the boiling water and cook for 3 minutes (or longer if you are using dried—follow the instructions on the package for cooking times). Drain the pasta, return it to the pan, and pour in the cavolo sauce.

Warm through over medium heat, using tongs to lift the pasta up toward you and working the sauce through thoroughly. Add your remaining pine nuts, season, and divide between two bowls. (Be warned—this can be a messy job with all that vibrant green sauce splashing about, so a little cleanup of your bowls before you serve might be in order.) Finish by topping each plate with some of the remaining Parmesan and a drizzle of olive oil.

Squid Ink Risotto, Lemon & Chile

Making squid ink risotto or pasta isn't as difficult as you think because you can easily buy squid ink packets from your fishmonger and keep them in the freezer. The lemon and chile give the dish a zesty lift. This is not your normal risotto, so don't reach for the Parmesan. The lemon and chile are what finish the dish.

SERVES 4
6½ cups [1.5 L] fish stock
½ cup [125 g] butter
3 tbsp extra-virgin olive oil, plus extra for drizzling
3 shallots, preferably banana shallots, finely diced
2 garlic cloves, finely chopped
2½ cups [500 g] risotto rice
3 tbsp [50 g] tomato paste
¾ cup plus 2 tbsp [200 ml] white wine
½ cup [125 ml] squid ink
2 pinches of dried chile flakes
1 lemon
Salt

Bring the fish stock to a simmer in a large pan.

In a separate pan, heat ¼ cup [50 g] of the butter and the olive oil together over medium heat. As soon as the butter starts foaming, add the shallots and garlic and cook for 5 minutes, or until they are soft but not colored.

Add the rice and turn up the heat slightly. Give it a good stir and cook for 2 minutes so that the grains of rice get coated in the butter and oil. Stir in the tomato paste and cook for a further 30 seconds, and then pour in the wine; the risotto should hiss as the wine hits the pan and then it will quiet down. Reduce the heat to a simmer and cook for 2 minutes. Add the squid ink and a pinch of chile flakes and give it a good stir.

Begin adding your hot fish stock, a ladle at a time, gently stirring as you go to aggravate the rice, allowing it to release its starch—this gives the risotto its lovely creamy consistency. →

Keep adding the stock, a ladle at a time, and stirring (they say you should only stir the rice in one direction). Make sure the stock has been absorbed each time before you add more. Continue until the rice is cooked, but still has a little bite to it (you may not need all the stock).

Remove the pan from the heat and stir in the remaining butter. Check the seasoning; it will need a touch of salt but not pepper as you already have heat from the chile flakes. Let the risotto rest for a couple of minutes. This gives the grains time to relax so the risotto will be less tense. You never want to serve a boiling risotto straight from the heat.

Divide the risotto among four plates. Give each plate a gentle tap from underneath, as this will help to flatten out the risotto, then grate some lemon zest over each plate. Add another pinch of chile flakes and a drizzle of extra-virgin olive oil.

Radicchio, Gorgonzola & Hazelnut Risotto

During a visit to Italy that involved an impromptu day in Venice, Tom, Rory, and I decided to do a tour of the *cicchetti* bars. These are Venetian wine bars that serve an array of different snacks, often served on bread, which are usually enjoyed from midmorning throughout the day. They are eaten standing up and with a small glass of local wine. It was glorious—well, it was raining, but an impromptu day in Venice is always a glorious thing.

Tom ended up deconstructing a few of those ingredient assemblies into his own dishes—this is one of them.

SERVES 4

6½ cups [1.5 L] vegetable stock
½ cup [125 g] butter
3 tbsp extra-virgin olive oil
3 shallots, preferably banana shallots, finely diced
2 garlic cloves, finely chopped
2½ cups [500 g] risotto rice
¾ cup plus 2 tbsp [200 ml] red wine
1⅓ cups [40 g] grated Parmesan
1 head of radicchio
Handful of flat-leaf parsley, coarsely chopped
4 oz [120 g] gorgonzola
½ cup [60 g] toasted hazelnuts, lightly crushed
Salt and freshly ground black pepper

Bring the vegetable stock to a simmer in a large pan.

In a separate pan, heat ¼ cup [50 g] of the butter and the olive oil together over medium heat. As soon as the butter starts foaming, add the shallots and garlic and cook for 5 minutes, or until they are soft but not colored.

Add the rice and turn up the heat slightly. Give it a good stir and cook for 2 minutes so that the grains of rice get coated in the butter and oil.

Pour in the wine; the risotto should hiss as the wine hits the pan and then it will quiet down. Reduce the heat to a simmer and cook for 2 minutes. →

Begin adding your hot vegetable stock, a ladle at a time, gently stirring as you go to aggravate the rice, allowing it to release its starch—this gives the risotto its lovely creamy consistency. Keep adding the stock, a ladle at a time, and stirring. Make sure the stock has been absorbed each time before you add more. Continue until the rice is cooked, but still has a little bite to it (you may not need all the stock). Remove the pan from the heat, stir in the remaining butter and the Parmesan, and season with salt and pepper.

Cut the radicchio lengthwise into quarters, and then shred into ¼-in [5-mm] slices; add to the risotto along with the chopped parsley. Let it rest for a minute or two.

When you're ready to serve, divide the risotto among four plates. Break the gorgonzola into small nuggets and scatter over the risotto, followed by the toasted hazelnuts.

Milk Risotto & San Daniele

A big part of how we cook is to always honor the architecture or shape of our ingredients: how they look and feel. So we don't like to mash or crush things too much, we don't like to dice herbs or vegetables. We like to keep things looking as much like themselves as possible, in the same way that adding the right amount of seasoning helps them taste more of themselves.

This risotto is one of those examples. We make the risotto, but instead of chopping up the ham, we leave the slices whole and place them over the cooked risotto. This way the fat melts in, and as you slice into the meat you get a good mouthfeel of salty, fatty meat, followed by silky milk risotto.

This is an ideal supper or lunch dish and can easily be scaled up or down.

SERVES 4

3 cups [750 ml] whole milk
3 cups [750 ml] chicken stock
½ cup [125 g] butter
3 tbsp extra-virgin olive oil
3 shallots, preferably banana shallots, finely diced
2 garlic cloves, finely chopped
2½ cups [500 g] risotto rice
¾ cup plus 2 tbsp [200 ml] white wine
1⅔ cups [50 g] Parmesan, grated, plus a little more to serve
6 oz [160 g] sliced prosciutto, preferably San Daniele
Salt and freshly ground black pepper

First put the milk and chicken stock in a large pan and bring to a simmer. In a separate pan, heat ¼ cup [50 g] of the butter and the oil together. As soon as the butter starts foaming, add the shallots and garlic and cook for 5 minutes, or until they are soft but not colored.

Add the rice and turn up the heat slightly. Give it a good stir and cook for 2 minutes so that the grains of rice get coated in the butter and oil.

Pour in the wine; the risotto should hiss as the wine hits the pan and will then quiet down (they say that this is because the rice is calling out for wine to cool it down). Reduce the heat to a simmer and cook for 2 minutes. Then, a ladle at a time, start adding the hot stock and milk to the rice, gently stirring as you go to aggravate the rice, allowing it to release its starch—this gives the risotto its lovely creamy consistency. Keep adding the stock, a ladle at a time, and stirring. Make sure it has been absorbed each time before you add more. Continue until the rice is cooked, but still has a little bite to it (you may not need all the stock).

Remove the pan from the heat, stir in the remaining butter and the Parmesan, and season with salt and pepper. Let the risotto rest for a couple of minutes. This gives the grains time to relax so the risotto will be less tense. You never want to serve a boiling risotto straight from the heat.

Divide the risotto among four plates, lay a few slices of prosciutto over the top, and finish with another little grating of Parmesan.

Autumn Squash, Garden Watercress, Sheep's Curd & Walnuts

Pumpkins and squash ease us colorfully from summer into autumn; the warm glow of their skins and flesh is a gentle transition into the darker days ahead. The textures and flavors in this dish work really well together to make a quick and easy dinner or lunch. We use the Italian rapini in the restaurant, but watercress works nicely.

Curd is a fresh cheese—the part you get when separating the curds and whey in cheesemaking. We use unpasteurized because you get a better flavor—you can buy it online or from most cheesemongers. If you can't get hold of it, then a good cottage cheese, preferably unpasteurized, is an acceptable alternative.

SERVES 2
18 oz [500 g] squash (butternut or any type of autumn squash)
¼ cup [50 g] butter
Extra-virgin olive oil
⅓ cup [40 g] walnuts, toasted and lightly crushed
Handful of watercress or rapini
Juice of ½ lemon
⅓ cup [80 g] sheep's or goat's curd (see page 317), or good cottage cheese
Salt and freshly ground black pepper

First peel the squash with a sharp peeler and cut into 2-in [5-cm] pieces.

Heat the butter with a glug of olive oil in a pan with a tight-fitting lid over medium-high heat. As soon as the butter starts to foam, add the squash and give it a stir.

Reduce the heat to medium and pop on the lid. Cook the squash, stirring every couple of minutes, for 8 to 10 minutes, or until the squash breaks down into almost a pulp. You may need to add a little water if it starts to stick, but this will evaporate as it cooks. Season the cooked squash and divide between two bowls.

Meanwhile, in a bowl, mix together the crushed walnuts, watercress, lemon juice, and some olive oil and season with salt and pepper. Spoon the curd over the squash and scatter the watercress-and-walnut mixture on and around the curd. Don't smother the curd or squash—you want to see the lovely colors underneath.

Slow down and relax, gently prepare your ingredients, pour yourself a glass of wine, put on some music, and enjoy a slower pace of cooking. These dishes are here to be cooked: some will be happy with a slow afternoon simmer and others will demand your full attention.

Slow-roasted Pork Belly & Pickled Rhubarb

Soon after Tom took over in the kitchen at Ducksoup, we had a massive pickling session. We ordered tons of fruit and vegetables and went on a pickling mission. We even made peach wine. We'd cooked pork belly for lunch, which we'd planned to have with green sauce, but when the sizzling pork came out of the oven, with its crispy skin and juicy fat, Tom said *that* would be perfect with pickled rhubarb, and we've not looked back.

SERVES 4
¾ cup [120 g] pickled rhubarb (see page 314)
3¼ lb [1.5 kg] pork belly (remove the bones in on-the-bone, but keep them)
Salt

Make the pickled rhubarb in advance, as it will keep for at least 1 week in an airtight container in the fridge. (Alternatively you can serve the pork belly with a spoonful of our green sauce; see page 35.)

Preheat the oven to 425°F [220°C]. Use a very sharp knife to score though the skin of the pork belly. The way we do this is to score where we want the portion slices to be, so if you're making dinner for four, then score eight sections, so that you have two pieces each. This will make it much easier to cut through once the pork is cooked, as you won't have to cut through that lovely, crackled pork skin.

Season the flesh-side of the pork belly with salt, and rest it on a rack on a roasting pan. Alternatively, you can rest the pork belly on the bones you removed—either way, you want to protect the meat from the intense heat coming off the base of the pan, which will make the edges dry. Season the skin-side of the pork with salt, rubbing it well into the skin. Leave the pork belly for 30 minutes; this will draw some liquid from the skin, helping to make it crispier. Place the pork belly in the oven and roast for 15 minutes, or until the skin starts to crackle. Then reduce the oven temperature to 325°F [165°C] and cook for a further hour, or until the meat is tender and the skin is crispy. Remove from the oven and allow to rest, uncovered, for 10 minutes.

To serve, slice the pork following your pre-scored lines. Place two pieces on each plate, overlapping slightly. Spoon the pickled rhubarb on and around the belly, and pour over a little of the pickling juices.

Ham Hock, Broth, Lima Beans & Greens

Broths appear fairly regularly on our menus—you can make them hearty or simple and light. We particularly like a good clean broth with subtle flavors to bring us out of winter, and this is one of those. Both the beans and the ham provide the protein, and so a little goes a long way. It's healthy, nourishing, and satisfying.

SERVES 4

5½ lb [2.5 kg] ham hocks
1 onion, coarsely chopped
2 carrots, coarsely chopped
1 leek, coarsely chopped
2 celery stalks, coarsely chopped
1 head of garlic, cut in half horizontally
2 fresh bay leaves
Few thyme sprigs
Few black peppercorns
3 cups [750 g] cooked lima beans (from a jar or can), drained
2 lb [1 kg] rapini, pointed-head cabbage, or spring greens
Extra-virgin olive oil
Crusty sourdough bread, to serve

Place the ham hock in your largest pan and cover with cold water. Bring to a boil over medium-high heat, then drain. Rinse out the pan, return the hock to the pan, and add plenty of cold water, making sure you fully cover the meat. This will remove any excess salt from the hock and saves you having to soak overnight or keep changing the water as you go.

Add the onion, carrot, leek, celery, garlic, herbs, and peppercorns to the hock and bring to a boil. Once boiling, reduce the heat to low and simmer for 2 to 3 hours, or until you can pull out the bone easily using a pair of tongs. You'll need to skim off any scum that forms on the surface, and you may need to top off the water.

When the hock is done, remove it from the pan and set aside. Strain the stock through a sieve into a clean pan and discard the vegetables. Bring the stock to a boil and then reduce the heat to a simmer— you want to reduce the stock by about a quarter. While the stock is reducing, return to the ham hock, which should now be cool enough to handle. Pull the meat from the bone in largeish chunks and discard both the bone and the skin.

Prepare the rapini by removing the last 2 in [5 cm] of the stalk and then cutting the leaves in half across, leaving them quite large because they will break down as they cook. Add to the reduced stock and cook for 1 minute, then add the drained lima beans and the ham hock pieces (and their juices) to the pan. Cook everything together for a further 2 minutes.

To serve, use tongs to pull out the rapini and place in the bottom of four bowls. Ladle the beans, meat, and broth over it. Finish with a splash of olive oil and serve with lots of crusty sourdough bread.

Gnudi 3 Ways

These great little ricotta dumplings—not to be confused with gnocchi, which are made using wheat flour and potatoes—are simple to make and take just a few minutes to cook. We can't recommend making gnudi enough, because everyone always loves it. We've chosen three of our favorite ways to serve gnudi here, although we are adding new ways with gnudi all the time. If you are having a few friends over, make gnudi!

SERVES 4
2 cups [500 g] ricotta
1 egg yolk
¼ cup [30 g] "00" flour
1 cup [30 g] grated Parmesan
Zest of 1 lemon
4½ cups [2 kg] semolina flour, for dusting (this seems a lot, but it can be reused)
Salt and freshly ground black pepper

Combine the ricotta, egg yolk, "00" flour, and Parmesan in a bowl, then add the lemon zest and salt and pepper and mix again.

In a large, deep, nonreactive baking pan or plastic container, spread out a layer of semolina flour about ¼ in [5 mm] thick.

Roll the gnudi mixture into 10 balls and then place them on the semolina flour in a single layer, making sure they do not touch. Repeat with the remaining gnudi mixture. Once you've used up all the mixture, cover the gnudi with the remaining semolina flour and chill in the fridge for 24 hours.

After 24 hours the semolina will have formed a crust on the gnudi— this helps the dumplings hold their shape.

When you're ready to cook the gnudi, bring a large pan of salted water to a boil, dust off the excess semolina flour (the excess semolina flour can be kept in the fridge and used again), and boil for 3 minutes. Follow one of the serving suggestions on the following pages.

1. Gnudi, Prosciutto & Parmesan

1 recipe gnudi (see page 204)
Extra-virgin olive oil
2⅔ cups [80 g] grated Parmesan
12 slices of prosciutto
Zest of ½ lemon
Freshly ground black pepper

Cook the gnudi as described on page 204. Remove from the pan and place in a large bowl with a ladleful of the cooking liquid, a good glug of olive oil, and half the Parmesan.

Give everything a gentle stir to create a sauce, and divide the gnudi equally among four plates. Spoon the sauce over and then lay the prosciutto on and around the gnudi in waves.

To serve, finish with the remaining Parmesan, a twist of black pepper, and a little lemon zest.

2. Gnudi & Wild Rabbit Ragu

4 rabbit legs
Extra-virgin olive oil
1 onion, diced
4 celery stalks, chopped
1 small fennel bulb, diced
1 head of garlic
7 oz [200 g] pancetta, chopped
2 bay leaves
Few rosemary sprigs
2¼ cups [500 ml] white wine
4½ cups [1 L] chicken stock
Parmesan rind, plus Parmesan for grating
Handful of flat-leaf parsley, leaves torn
1 recipe gnudi (see page 204)
Salt and freshly ground black pepper

Preheat the oven to 325°F [160°C].

Place a large frying pan over medium-high heat. Rub the rabbit legs
with oil and season with salt and pepper, then brown for 5 minutes
on each side, or until golden brown. Remove from the frying pan
and put into a large roasting pan. Add a little more olive oil to the
pan and fry the vegetables, garlic, pancetta, and herbs for 5 minutes,
or until soft and golden. Pour in the wine and reduce for 2 minutes.
Then add the stock and Parmesan rind and bring to a boil.

Once the liquid has come to a boil, pour it over the rabbit legs, cover
the pan tightly with foil, and braise in the oven for 1½ hours, after
which time the rabbit will be cooked and should fall off the bone.
Remove the rabbit legs from the pan and set aside to cool slightly.
Pour the remaining sauce into a clean pan and place over low heat.
Put another pan of salted water on to boil for the gnudi. When the
rabbit is cool enough to handle, remove the meat from the bones
in good-sized chunks and add to the sauce along with the parsley.

Cook the gnudi in boiling water for 3 minutes, then remove from
the pan and add to the ragu. Give the pan a gentle shake to combine
and cook over low heat for 2 minutes. Divide the gnudi among four
large bowls, ladle any remaining ragu over it, and finish with some
grated Parmesan and a drizzle of extra-virgin olive oil.

3. Gnudi, Watercress & Goat's Curd

1 recipe gnudi (see page 204)
⅓ cup [80 g] butter
6 tbsp [100 ml] extra-virgin olive oil, plus extra for drizzling
Large bunch of watercress, thick stalks removed
⅔ cup [160 g] goat's curd (see page 317) or good-quality cottage cheese,
    preferably unpasteurized
Zest of 1 lemon
Salt and freshly ground black pepper

Bring a large pan of salted water to a boil and cook the gnudi as
described on page 204, reserving some of the cooking liquid, as you'll
need it for your sauce.

Heat the butter and olive oil together in a large pan until the butter
begins to foam. Add the watercress and a couple small ladles of the
gnudi cooking water and stir gently. As soon as the watercress starts
to wilt, add the goat's curd or cottage cheese and give it another stir
(you may need to add a little more of the gnudi water to thin the
sauce slightly).

Drain the gnudi and add to the sauce. Give everything a gentle stir,
being careful not to break the gnudi. Divide the gnudi and sauce
among four bowls and finish each bowl with a grating of lemon zest,
a good drizzle of olive oil, and a few twists of black pepper.

Fritto Misto & Saffron Mayo

This was a dish we opened with: the sun was shining, the doors were open, and there was this beautifully presented fritto misto with artichokes and sliced orange all in the mix. Not many people like to deep-fry at home, but the result is worth it. And, with a side serving of saffron mayo and a glass of rosé, this is summer all over.

SERVES 4

⅓ cup [100 g] saffron mayo (see page 47)
4 long-stem artichokes
Pinch of dried chile flakes
1 bay leaf
2 medium squid, cleaned (ask your fishmonger)
1 blood orange
2 cups [250 g] "00" flour
1½ cups [250 g] fine semolina
2¼ cups [500 ml] milk
Grapeseed or sunflower oil, for frying
4 raw shell-on shrimp
4 wild sea bass fillets, about 4 oz [100 g] each
2 lemons
Salt

First make your saffron mayo, following the instructions given on page 47. Set aside in the fridge until ready to use.

Start by prepping the artichokes as described on page 79. Place in a pan and cover with cold water, add the chile flakes, bay leaf, and a pinch of salt, and bring to a boil. Reduce the heat to a simmer and cook for 6 minutes; drain and set to one side.

Meanwhile, open up your squid by inserting a knife into the body and cutting along one side. Clean away any membrane left inside and pat dry with paper towels. Open the squid body out into a rectangle and cut into three pieces. Cut the tentacles in half from top to bottom and pat dry.

Slice the blood orange, unpeeled, crosswise into 8 slices and set aside. →

Get everything ready for coating and frying your fritto misto—you will need to cook in batches, so it's important to do everything in the right order. Mix together the flour and semolina in a large bowl and add a pinch of salt. Pour the milk into a large, shallow bowl and set aside. Pour the oil into a large, heavy-bottomed pan and heat to 350°F [180°C]—to test this drop in a small cube of bread; if it sizzles and turns golden in 10 seconds, the oil is ready. Alternatively, if you have a deep fryer, simply set the temperature to 350°F [180°C]. Preheat the oven to 275°F [140°C] and line a large baking pan with a tea towel (one that you don't mind getting covered in oil).

Start with artichokes and orange slices; once they're cooked they'll happily wait for the other ingredients. Using kitchen tongs, dip the artichokes and orange slices into the flour mix, then into the milk, and then back into the flour mix. Then, a few pieces at a time, place them in the hot oil and cook for 4 minutes before removing and draining in the lined pan. Season with a little salt and pop the pan in the oven to keep them warm.

Repeat the process of flour, milk, flour with the shrimp and fry them for 5 minutes, then drain, season with salt, and add to the pan in the oven. Repeat with the sea bass fillets—they will take 3 minutes to cook. Finally, repeat with the squid, cooking for 2 minutes.

Once everything is cooked, transfer to a large serving platter, scattering everything randomly so it all falls very naturally. Cut the lemons into wedges and tuck in and around the fritto misto. Serve with the saffron mayo on the side.

Grilled Lamb Leg 3 Ways

There is a stunning vineyard in the Bekaa Valley on the road from Damascus to Aleppo called Chateau Massaya that also has a restaurant situated among the vines. You arrive early and watch as lunch builds: Fires are lit, bowls of mouth-watering tomatoes, beans, salads, labneh, and breads appear. Soups are warmed over the fire and pots bubble away. Guests ebb and flow toward the table and the flames as they slowly satiate themselves throughout the afternoon. It's one of the most peaceful places I have visited. And it was here that I first properly discovered labneh. They paired it with grilled meats and gently roasted vegetables and poached fruits. This dish is inspired by that visit; here we have given three of our favorite ways with lamb and labneh.

The charring gives an added dimension of flavor to the meat, so if you can char it and then finish it in the oven, that is the ideal. Alternatively, cook it on a grill.

SERVES 4–6
4½- to 5½-lb [2- to 2.5-kg] lamb leg, boned and butterflied (ask your butcher)
Olive oil
Salt and freshly ground black pepper

Preheat the oven to 400°F [200°C].

Heat a large grill pan (big enough to hold your lamb) until it is smoking.

Rub the oil into the lamb and season with salt and pepper. Place in the grill pan and cook for 5 minutes on one side. You may need to turn the heat down a tad, as there will be a lot of smoke. Turn the lamb over and cook for 5 minutes on the other side. Then, using a pair of tongs, turn the meat onto its side and cook the edges for 3 minutes on each side.

The lamb should now have lovely grill marks and a good smoky flavor to it. If you're cooking this in summer you can also get the same effect on the barbecue. →

Once all the sides of your meat are sealed, transfer to a large roasting pan and roast for 16 to 18 minutes for a medium lamb leg and a bit longer for a larger leg. You want the meat blushing with a pink color as opposed to being rare. To check if your meat is cooked, after 16 to 18 minutes give it a gentle prod with your finger on the largest part. It should have a little bounce to it but should still feel a little firm. If there is little resistance, then it's undercooked, so give it another 3 to 4 minutes.

When the meat is cooked, remove it from the oven and let it rest for around 15 minutes, covered loosely with foil. This is important, as it gives the meat a chance to relax and get the juices flowing, and it means the meat will stay moist when you come round to slicing it.

When you come to carve the meat, rather than cutting directly across, slice the meat at about a 30-degree angle, which makes slightly triangular chunks, creating more texture to the meat.

Follow one of the serving suggestions on the following pages.

1. Grilled Lamb Leg, Labneh, Fava Beans & Za'atar

1 recipe grilled lamb leg (see page 212)
4½ lb [2 kg] fava beans in the pod
¼ cup [35 g] sesame seeds
2 tbsp sumac
2 tbsp dried wild oregano
Extra-virgin olive oil
Juice of 1 lemon
¾ cup [200 g] labneh (see page 323)
Salt

While the lamb is resting, bring a large pan of salted water to a boil while you shell the fava beans. Cook the beans for just 1 minute, then drain and refresh in cold water. If your fava beans are on the large side, it's best to skin them; otherwise, they can be a little bitter and chewy. Simply pinch off their tops and squeeze the bean from the skin.

To make the za'atar, toast the sesame seeds in a dry frying pan for 3 to 4 minutes, giving them a toss as you go, until the seeds turn a golden brown. Add to a bowl with the sumac, dried oregano, and a good pinch of salt and mix together. Set aside.

Gently warm a good glug of the oil in a frying pan and add the fava beans, lemon juice, and a pinch of salt. Warm through for 2 to 3 minutes.

To serve, lay the lamb pieces out on a platter, randomly and so that they don't cover the whole plate (you want to see white space). Spoon the labneh in and around the lamb and scatter your fava beans over the top, pouring over the lemony oil you have cooked them in. Finish by sprinkling the za'atar over all. You can also serve on individual plates if you prefer.

2. Grilled Lamb Leg, Labneh & Poached Apricots

1 recipe grilled lamb leg (see page 212)
Extra-virgin olive oil
8 fresh apricots, unpitted
Few thyme leaves
¾ cup [200 g] labneh (see page 323)
Juice of 1 lemon
Salt

As soon as you put the lamb into the oven, place an ovenproof frying pan over medium heat and add a dash of oil. Once your oil is hot, add the apricots and blister for 5 minutes, shaking the pan to move them around, until the skin starts to blister. Add the thyme leaves, transfer the pan to the oven, and roast for 8 to 10 minutes, or until the fruit is cooked but is still a little firm (they should still hold their shape). Set aside to cool while you carve the lamb as described on page 214.

Arrange the pieces of lamb randomly over a serving platter (or individual plates). When the apricots are cool enough to handle, tear them open and place them in and around the lamb. Do the same with spoonfuls of the labneh, then squeeze over the lemon juice. Drizzle with olive oil and season with a little pinch of salt.

3. Grilled Lamb Leg, Labneh & Pomegranate

1 recipe grilled lamb leg (see page 212)
1 large pomegranate
¾ cup [200 g] labneh (see page 323)
Small handful of mint leaves
Extra-virgin olive oil

While the lamb is resting, remove the seeds from the pomegranate by cutting it in half and then holding it over a bowl, cut-side down on your spread palm. Hit the back of the pomegranate with a wooden spoon or rolling pin so that the seeds drop out into the bowl. If you have trouble, try turning the half inside out and gently coaxing the remaining seeds out with your fingers.

Carve the lamb as described on page 214 and arrange on a serving platter (or individual plates). Spoon the labneh on and around the lamb and scatter the pomegranate seeds over all, along with any juice from the bowl. Tear and scatter over the mint leaves, and finish with a glug of olive oil.

Vitello Tonnato

Vitello tonnato is possibly one of our all-time favorite flavor combinations. Tonnato is a tuna mayonnaise, and a Piedmontese classic. It's usually served as cold, thin slices of veal, with the tuna mayo spooned over. We've upped the ante on ours with the addition of anchovies and capers. We also use veal sirloin to give the dish more texture. This is a summer classic, best served at room temperature.

SERVES 4

¾ cup [200 g] mayonnaise (see page 47)
1¾ lb [800 g] piece pasture-raised veal sirloin
Extra-virgin olive oil
11 oz [300 g] good-quality canned tuna in oil
8 salt-packed anchovy fillets
Juice of 1 lemon
2 tbsp small capers
Salt and freshly ground black pepper

First prepare your mayonnaise following the instructions given on page 47. You can make this a few days in advance, as it will keep well in the fridge in an airtight container. Preheat the oven to 400°F [200°C] and heat a grill pan until smoking. Rub the veal with oil and season well with salt and pepper. Cook in the grill pan for 6 minutes on each side to sear the meat and give it a smoky, charred flavor. Transfer to a roasting pan and cook in the oven for 12 minutes. Remove from the oven, cover loosely with foil, and allow to rest and cool for 10 to 12 minutes.

Meanwhile, make the sauce. Put the mayonnaise, 3½ oz [100 g] of the tuna, the anchovies, and the lemon juice into a food processor and blend until smooth. Add a couple of tablespoons of water to loosen the mayonnaise a little—it should have a saucelike consistency. Once the meat has cooled (you want it to be warm to the touch, rather than hot), cut it into thick slices on a slight angle, almost like wedges. Lay them over a large serving platter, and then spoon the sauce on and around the veal. Don't completely cover the veal; you want to be able to see the beautiful veal meat coming though.

To finish, crumble the remaining tuna over the top, scatter the capers over, and give it a good drizzle of olive oil and a few twists of black pepper.

Braised Oxtail & Wet Polenta

Polenta is a great platform for so many things and soaks up all your tasty juices. We pair it with wild mushrooms or pot-roasted birds, and on a recent trip to Italy we even had it with fritto misto. Polenta takes hours to cook from scratch; you can't leave it standing for a minute or it will stick, so someone always has to be stirring the pot (you can always tell who it is because they glow red hot with sweaty faces). We find this very labor-intensive, so we prefer to buy good-quality quick-cook polenta instead. This is by far one of our favorite winter dishes—sometimes it appears as a smaller dish on the bar menu, other times as a main dish.

This is an ideal all-in-one dish: you don't need anything else, so it's good as a winter night's supper or late Sunday lunch, curled up by the fire with a large glass of wine.

SERVES 4

3¼-lb [1.5-kg] jointed oxtail
Olive oil
1 large onion, coarsely chopped
1 lb [500 g] carrots, coarsely chopped
1 head of garlic, cut in half horizontally
4 fresh bay leaves
Few thyme sprigs
Pinch of dried chile flakes
½ cup [125 g] tomato paste
1½ cups [375 ml] red wine
6½ cups [1.5 L] veal or beef stock
4½ cups [1 L] whole milk
1½ cups [200 g] quick-cooking polenta
¼ cup [50 g] butter
2⅔ cups [80 g] Parmesan, grated, plus extra to finish
Salt and freshly ground black pepper

Preheat the oven to 325°F [160°C].

Place a large pan over medium heat. Rub the oxtail with olive oil and then season with salt and pepper. Sear on all sides in the pan until nicely caramelized—you're looking for a good brown color. Once browned, transfer to a roasting pan big enough to hold the oxtail and the sauce to come. →

Leaving the oxtail fat in the pan, add the onion, carrots, and garlic and cook until caramelized, stirring every so often—this will take about 10 minutes. Add the herbs, chile flakes, and tomato paste and cook for a further 2 minutes.

Pour in the wine to deglaze the pan and let it bubble and simmer for 2 minutes. After the wine has had a chance to boil away, add the stock and return to a boil. Once boiling, pour the sauce over the oxtail. Cover the roasting pan tightly with foil and cook in the oven for 3 hours, or until the meat is falling off the bone (check the biggest bone to test this).

Once the oxtail is cooked, leave it to sit for half an hour and then remove the meat from the sauce and set aside. Pass the sauce through a sieve into a clean pan, pressing all the vegetables to get as much juice and flavor as you can. By the time you have done this the meat should be cool enough to handle. Remove the meat from the bone and return it to your sauce, making sure you discard any fatty bits that are attached to the larger bones. Gently heat the sauce and use a ladle to skim off any fat that appears around the top of the sauce. Keep on a simmer to reduce the sauce by a third, then keep warm while you make the polenta.

Pour the milk into a large pan and heat until it is just scalded. Pour the polenta into the hot milk in a steady stream, whisking as you go. Keep whisking over medium heat until the polenta thickens and starts to come away from the side of the pan; this will take about 3 minutes.

When the polenta has thickened to the consistency of lightly whipped cream, add the butter and Parmesan and season with salt and pepper. It will take a lot of seasoning, so keep tasting to make sure you've added enough. Stir everything together; if the polenta starts thickening, add a little more milk, as you want it to be a bit loose and to wobble when you shake the pan.

When you are ready to serve, pour the polenta into four bowls, then top with the oxtail sauce, making sure you don't cover all the polenta. Finish each bowl with a generous grating of Parmesan.

Roast Hake, Fennel, Orange & Almond Aïoli

Roasting hake on the bone like this keeps it beautiful and moist. Hake has a similar texture to cod (which you could also use here) but is more flavorsome. This makes a satisfying main course, and would suit a weekend when you've had time to visit the fishmonger and get some fresh fish.

SERVES 4

⅔ cup [200 g] aïoli (see page 47)
Extra-virgin olive oil
4 hake or cod steaks on the bone, 9 to 10 oz [250 to 300 g] each
2 fennel bulbs, cut into ⅜-in [1-cm] slices, fronds retained
4 unpeeled garlic cloves, smashed
1 large orange, cut into ¼-in [5-mm] slices
1 tsp dried chile flakes
¾ cup [100 g] toasted sliced almonds
Juice of 1 lemon
Salt

First make the aïoli—you can do this in advance, as it will keep in the fridge in an airtight container for up to 5 days.

Preheat the oven to 400°F [200°C].

Heat a little olive oil in a large frying pan over medium heat until just smoking. Season the hake steaks with salt and then fry flesh-side down for 3 minutes, or until golden; turn and repeat on the other side. Transfer the seared steaks to a large baking pan and set to one side.

Add a touch more oil to the pan, and add the fennel slices and garlic cloves. Cook until nicely colored, 5 to 6 minutes, and then add to the hake pan. Add the orange slices and cook for 1 minute on each side, or until they start to caramelize. Add to the hake, season with a little more salt, sprinkle with the chile flakes, and pour a good glug of olive oil over the top. →

Bake for 8 to 10 minutes, or until the fish is cooked and starting to come away from the bone and the fennel is cooked but still retains a little bite.

Meanwhile, crush the toasted sliced almonds in a mortar and pestle so they're ground but still hold some texture (you are not looking for powder). Stir into the aïoli and decant into a pretty bowl.

Once the fish is ready, squeeze the lemon juice over it and scatter with the fennel fronds. Serve straight from the pan, adding a dollop of almond aïoli to each plate.

Roast Hake, Mussels, Charred Sourdough & Saffron Aïoli

This dish comes from the time when Tom worked with Mitch Tonks; I would also go and visit Mitch and his wife, Penny, down in Brixham where they live. Mitch is the ultimate food obsessive— I don't think I have ever met anyone quite as passionate about food and restaurants as him. He has a memory for nearly every dish he's ever eaten, it would seem, and one of his great loves was eating bouillabaisse in Marseille. This is our tribute to him. It's not a bouillabaisse in the true sense, but like one, the hard work is in the stock, although you can cheat slightly by using a really good shellfish soup from your fishmonger.

SERVES 4

2 lb [1 kg] mussels
4 hake or cod steaks, about 12 oz
    [350 g] each
Extra-virgin olive oil
Handful of flat-leaf parsley,
    coarsely chopped
Juice of 1 lemon
Salt and freshly ground black pepper

To serve
⅔ cup [160 g] aïoli (see page 47)
Pinch of saffron threads
4 slices of sourdough bread

For the crab stock
3¼ lb [1.5 kg] frozen whole crabs
Extra-virgin olive oil
4 celery stalks, coarsely chopped
1 large onion, skin on and
    coarsely chopped
1 head of garlic, cut in half
    horizontally
1 lb [500 g] carrots, coarsely chopped
Few sprigs of thyme
3 bay leaves
1 tbsp fennel seeds
1 tbsp black peppercorns
½ cup [150 g] tomato paste
¾ cup [150 g] rice

First make the crab stock. Preheat the oven to 350°F [180°C]. Smash up the crabs into small pieces, lay them flat on a roasting pan, and bake for 45 minutes, until nicely browned.

Meanwhile, heat a glug of olive oil in a pan over medium-high heat, and cook the vegetables for 8 to 10 minutes, stirring occasionally, until they begin to caramelize. Add the bay leaves, fennel seeds, peppercorns, and tomato paste and cook for a further 5 minutes.

Add the crab pieces and deglaze the roasting pan with water so that no flavor is wasted. Add 4 qt [4 L] of water and bring up to a boil, skimming off any scum that appears. Reduce the heat and simmer gently for 3 hours.

226

At this point, add the rice—it will help thicken the stock—and then simmer for a further hour. Take the stock off the heat and, once it is cool enough, pass it through a sieve.

Prepare the aïoli as described on page 47 and set aside in the fridge until needed (you can make this a couple of days in advance).

Rinse the mussels well under cold water, removing any beards by pulling them sharply toward you. Discard any shells that do not close firmly when tapped with the back of a knife.

Preheat the oven to 425°F [220°C]. Place a large frying pan over medium-high heat while you oil the fish steaks and season with salt. Sear the fish for 3 minutes on each side, then remove from the pan and place in a roasting pan.

Pour 4½ cups [1 L] of your crab stock into the frying pan and bring to a boil; pour over the fish in the roasting pan. Scatter the mussels in and around the fish, tucking them into the stock. Bake, uncovered, for 8 to 10 minutes, or until the mussels have all opened up (discard any that remain closed after this time).

Meanwhile, soak the saffron threads for the aïoli in a tablespoon of warm water for 5 minutes to "bleed." Stir this saffron water into your aïoli. Heat a grill pan until smoking while you brush the sourdough slices with olive oil. Char on both sides (you can also do this in a toaster).

Remove the baked fish from the oven. Scatter the parsley over it, squeeze over the lemon juice, and give your pan a good shake to mix everything up.

Place the sourdough around the edges of the roasting pan and spoon a dollop of saffron aïoli onto each piece. Drizzle the whole thing with olive oil and take the pan to the table, with the bowl of aïoli so that people can add more if they wish.

Roast Poussin in Milk, Shallots & Sage

We love cooking chicken and poussin this way. Imagine all those tasty juices being soaked up into the milk, which is keeping your meat soft and tender. As you eat it you'll want to spoon up every last drop until your plate is clean.

SERVES 4

4 poussins
Olive oil
9 oz [250 g] round shallots, peeled
2¼ cups [500 ml] chicken stock
2¼ cups [500 ml] whole milk
1 bunch of sage
Salt and freshly ground black pepper

Preheat the oven to 410°F [210°C].

First spatchcock the poussins. Place each poussin breast-side down on a cutting board and use sharp kitchen scissors to cut down either side of the backbone. Remove the backbone, turn the poussin over, and then push down hard on the breastbone to flatten it out.

Season the birds with salt and pepper and rub with a little olive oil. Place a large, heavy-bottomed frying pan over high heat and brown the birds one at a time, until golden on all sides. Transfer the birds to a deep roasting pan.

In the same frying pan, fry the shallots for just 2 to 3 minutes, or until golden, then add to the pan with the poussins.

Pour the chicken stock into the pan to deglaze it: let it bubble while you scrape the bottom of the pan. Add the milk and then tear in the sage leaves. Pour the whole mixture over the poussins—the liquid should come about halfway up the poussins.

Roast the birds for 20 to 25 minutes. As the milk cooks in the oven, it curdles into a cheese-like consistency.

Allow the birds to rest for 5 minutes before transferring to a serving platter. Spoon the sauce over them and serve.

Crispy Lamb, Labneh, Mint, Red Onion & Pomegranate

I think the combination of ingredients here makes a near perfect salad—there is just enough (but not too much) crispy meat to give the dish depth and that umami flavor, and pairing it with the cool labneh, fresh mint, onion, and pomegranate seeds keeps the flavors clean and fresh. Lamb breast is a great, cheap cut, but you can also use any leftover lamb shoulder you might have from another recipe you've cooked on the weekend. This works as a starter dish or main course salad, or as part of a sharing feast.

SERVES 4

1 whole lamb breast, about 4½ lb [2 kg], cut in half
2¼ cups [500 ml] lamb stock
1 pomegranate
Extra-virgin olive oil
1 tsp dried chile flakes
Small handful of mint leaves
Small handful of flat-leaf parsley
1 red onion, thinly sliced
Juice of 1 lemon
⅔ cup [160 g] labneh (see page 323)
Grilled flatbread or toasted sourdough bread, to serve
Salt and freshly ground black pepper

Preheat the oven to 325°F [160°C]. Season the lamb breast with salt and pepper and put it into a large roasting pan. Pour the lamb stock over it, cover tightly with foil, and bake for 2 to 3 hours, or until the meat easily comes away from the bone.

Once cooked, remove the lamb breast from the stock and allow to cool. Keep the lamb stock, as you can use it another day—simply pour it into small containers and freeze.

While the lamb cools, remove the seeds from the pomegranate by cutting it in half and then holding it over a bowl, cut-side down on your spread palm. Hit the back of the pomegranate with a wooden spoon or rolling pin so that the seeds drop out into the bowl. If you have trouble, try turning the half inside out and gently coaxing the remaining seeds out with your fingers. →

Once the lamb breast is cool enough to handle, remove all the meat from the bones in large chunks and set aside. Heat a frying pan over medium-high heat and add a generous glug of oil. Add the chile flakes and then fry the lamb until nice and crisp, giving it a pinch of salt as it cooks.

When the lamb is crisp, transfer to a large bowl. Tear in the mint and parsley and add the sliced onion. Squeeze in the lemon juice, add another good splash of olive oil and half the pomegranate seeds, and season with salt and pepper.

Toss everything together with your hands and then gently coax the salad out of the bowl with your fingers onto individual plates. Spoon a dollop of labneh onto a third of the plate and finish by scattering the entire dish with pomegranate seeds. Serve with grilled flatbread or toasted sourdough.

Slow Roast Pork Belly, Kale & Arrocina Beans

The tender and gelatinous texture of slow-cooked pork is a warm and satisfying thing to eat on a winter's afternoon or evening. The beans provide the starch in this dish, making it a good all-in-one with no need for sides, while the kale gives you your daily portion of greens. Arrocina beans are small, white beans that hold their shape and texture well when cooked—you can buy them online from good specialist suppliers, although cannellini beans can be used instead.

SERVES 4

2 lb [1 kg] pork belly, skin removed
6 tbsp [100 ml] olive oil
1 onion, diced
2 garlic cloves, sliced
4 fresh bay leaves
¾ cup [200 ml] dry sherry
3 tbsp sherry vinegar
6½ cups [1.5 L] chicken stock
9 oz [250 g] arrocina beans, soaked in
   cold water overnight
1 lb [500 g] green kale
Salt and freshly ground black pepper

For the sourdough crumbs
2½ cups [100 g] stale sourdough bread,
   crusts removed, torn into small pieces
1 garlic clove, crushed
Few thyme sprigs
¼ cup [60 ml] extra-virgin olive oil
Pinch of salt

Preheat the oven to 325°F [160°C]. Cut the pork belly into 2-in [5-cm] squares and season with salt and pepper.

Heat the olive oil in a large, heavy-bottomed pan over medium heat. Once hot, sear the pork belly on all sides until golden brown. Remove from the pan with a slotted spoon (leaving the oil in the pan) and set to one side.

In the same pan, cook the onion, garlic, and bay leaves over medium heat for about 8 minutes, or until soft, stirring so that the onion doesn't catch and burn. Pour in the sherry and let it bubble and deglaze the pan, then add the sherry vinegar. Simmer for about 2 minutes to cook off the alcohol. Pour in the chicken stock.

Drain the beans and tip them into a casserole dish that is big enough to hold all the beans, pork, and stock. Scatter the seared pork belly over the beans and pour over the onion-sherry-stock mixture. →

233

Cover with a tight-fitting lid or seal with parchment paper and a double layer of foil to keep in all the flavor. Bake for 2 hours, or until the pork is tender and the beans are cooked.

While the pork is in the oven, you can make the sourdough crumbs. Put the bread pieces in a bowl with the garlic, the leaves from the thyme sprigs, the olive oil, and a good pinch of salt. Give it a good mix so that the bread soaks up the oil and garlic, then spread out on a baking pan and bake them in the oven with the pork for about 15 minutes, or until the crumbs are golden and crispy. They will need a shake or turn halfway through cooking.

Bring a pan of salted water to a boil. Tear the leaves from the kale stalks and cook the leaves in the boiling water for 30 seconds. Drain and refresh under cold water; once cold, squeeze out as much excess water as possible and set aside.

When the pork is cooked, remove the lid or parchment and foil covering (take care, as a lot of steam will come out as you do this). Stir in the blanched kale. Top with the sourdough crumbs and serve straight from the pot.

Baked Lamb Kibbeh, Cucumber & Mint Yogurt

Kibbeh is a popular dish in Middle Eastern countries, a blend of bulgur wheat, onion, and minced lean beef, lamb, goat, or even camel meat. It's a kind of deep-fried croquette—a wheat-coated, stuffed spiced meat, although sometimes it's just the meat shaped by hand into balls or torpedo shapes and baked or cooked in broth. Tom tried a few patty versions, but none of them ended up quite how they should have, so he instead he went for the more "pielike" version, which he served on plates with a dollop of cucumber yogurt and some mint leaves. Cooking it this way means the lamb unleashes its juicy flavor into the spices, and the crisp wheat topping combined with the cooling yogurt makes a happy marriage. This is a great feast dish, ideal as a starter for six or as a main dish for four.

SERVES 6 AS A STARTER, OR 4 AS A MAIN DISH
3¼ cups [500 g] bulgur wheat
¾ cup [200 ml] olive oil
1 tbsp cumin seeds
1 tbsp coriander seeds
1 tbsp nigella seeds
1 tbsp dried chile flakes
1 tbsp paprika
½ tbsp ground cinnamon
1 onion, diced
2 garlic cloves, chopped
¾ cup [100 g] toasted pine nuts
2½ lb [1.25 kg] ground lamb
Cucumber yogurt (see page 169), to serve
Handful of mint leaves, to serve
Salt and freshly ground black pepper

Soak the bulgur wheat in 4½ cups [1 L] boiling water (from a kettle) for 1 hour.

Preheat the oven to 400°F [200°C] and lightly oil a round, deep-sided ovenproof dish, about 12 in [30 cm] in diameter.

Heat the olive oil in a frying pan over very low heat and add the whole spices and chile flakes. Temper the spices for about 5 minutes—this helps to wake them up. Add the paprika, cinnamon, and onion and cook for a further 12 minutes, or until the onion is soft and translucent. Add the garlic and pine nuts and cook for 2 minutes.

Turn up the heat to medium-high and add 2 lb [1 kg] of the ground lamb to the pan and season with salt and pepper. Cook for 8 minutes, breaking up the meat, until it is browned on all sides, then remove from the heat and allow to cool.

Meanwhile, make the bulgur topping. Rinse and drain the soaked bulgur, squeezing out as much moisture as you can. Add to a food processor with the remaining 8 oz [250 g] ground lamb and a pinch of salt. Blend until you have a smooth paste.

Line your oiled baking dish with two-thirds of the bulgur mixture, to a thickness of about ¼ in [5 mm], patting it against the sides of the dish to form a shallow wall that will help encase the lamb mixture. Pour in the lamb, spread it evenly over the base, and then cover with the remaining bulgur mixture. The best way to do this is by flattening out pieces of the bulgur mixture and then sticking them together over the top of the lamb.

Bake the kibbeh for 30 minutes, or until golden brown and the juices from the lamb are bubbling around the sides.

Serve straight from the dish and spoon out portions onto plates—just as you might a shepherd's pie. Add a generous helping of the cucumber yogurt and tear over the fresh mint leaves.

Wild Boar Ragu

Wild boar will give a much more intense, gamy flavor to your ragu; it's also much leaner than pork so is good to use once in a while if you get the chance. However, good pork will do just as well—just make sure it is well reared, and always buy local. This is a warming dish to treat a few friends to on a winter weekend evening: full of aromatic herbs, red wine, and that intense pork flavor.

SERVES 4

2 tbsp olive oil
9 oz [250 g] pancetta, cut into lardons
1¾ lb [750 g] wild boar or pork shoulder, cut in ¼-in [5-mm] dice
Pinch of fennel seeds
1 onion, diced
2 celery stalks, chopped
2 carrots, diced
Handful of sage leaves, coarsely chopped
2 rosemary sprigs
4 fresh bay leaves
Pinch of dried chile flakes
4 garlic cloves, chopped
2 tbsp tomato paste
2¼ cups [500 ml] good red wine
4½ cups [1 L] beef stock
Small handful of flat-leaf parsley, coarsely chopped
2⅔ cups [80 g] Parmesan, grated
12 oz [320 g] fresh pasta (see page 45), or use dried
Salt and freshly ground black pepper

Preheat the oven to 325°F [160°C].

Place a large stockpot with a tight-fitting lid over medium-high heat. Add the olive oil and fry the pancetta for 5 minutes, or until golden brown. Remove with a slotted spoon and set aside, leaving all the fatty juices behind.

Season the wild boar or pork shoulder with salt and pepper and cook in the same pan in pancetta fat for 8 minutes, stirring every now and then, until the meat is seared all over. Remove with a slotted spoon and add to the pancetta. By now the oil will have lots of flavor ready for the next stage. →

Add the fennel seeds to the pan and temper for 1 minute over medium-low heat. Add the onion, celery, carrots, herbs, and chile flakes and cook over medium heat until everything has softened, about 12 minutes. Add the garlic and cook for 2 minutes (you don't want to add the garlic too early; otherwise, it will burn).

Stir in the tomato paste and cook for 2 minutes, then pour in the wine, letting it bubble and reduce for 5 minutes. Pour in the beef stock and then return all the meat with its juices to the pan. Bring to a boil, then turn down the heat to a low simmer and cook for 1½ hours, or until the meat is tender, stirring once in a while to make sure it doesn't stick (you may need a little water if it looks like it is drying out). Alternatively, pour everything into a lidded casserole and bake for 1½ hours.

When you're almost ready to serve, bring a large pan of salted water to a boil for your pasta. Once the ragu is ready, remove it from the heat and stir in the parsley and about half of the Parmesan. Taste and adjust the seasoning (it's best to do this at the end of the cooking time because the ragu will become saltier as it reduces, especially if you're using pancetta).

Cook the pasta for 3 minutes (or follow the instructions on the package if using dried), drain, and add to the ragu. Give it a good mix and serve with some crusty bread and the remaining Parmesan in a bowl alongside.

Salted Beef Cheek, Cucumber, Peas & Horseradish

One of our favorite salads, this works well as a starter or as part of a sharing feast, or just as a supper for 2 or 4. The crispy, slightly salty beef cheek is perfectly balanced against the cool cucumber and peas, with a little heat from the fresh horseradish.

You will need to simmer the beef cheeks for a few hours, but once they are cooked this recipe is really simple.

SERVES 4

1 lb [500 g] salted beef cheeks or brisket
1 carrot, halved
1 onion, quartered
2 celery stalks
1 head of garlic, sliced in half horizontally
2 bay leaves
Few thyme sprigs
1 tsp black peppercorns
2 lb [1 kg] peas in the pod, or 8 oz [250 g] frozen peas
Extra-virgin olive oil
2 mini cucumbers
Juice of 1 lemon
¼-in [5-mm] piece of fresh horseradish
Salt and freshly ground black pepper

Place the beef cheeks in a large pan of water over medium-high heat. As soon as the water comes to a boil, drain the cheeks in a colander and wash out the pan (this is a quick way to remove the salt from the cheeks and saves you having to soak them overnight).

Place the drained cheeks back into the clean pan and cover generously with fresh water. Add the carrot, onion, celery, garlic, bay leaves, thyme, and peppercorns and bring to a boil, then reduce to a low simmer and cook for 2 to 3 hours, or until the cheeks are tender. Add water if the meat becomes exposed. Test the cheeks by squeezing them with a pair of tongs—they should break up easily.

Drain the beef cheeks (keep the cooking liquid, as it will make a great base for a soup and can be stored in the freezer). Set the cheeks aside to cool. →

Bring a large pan of salted boiled water to a boil while you shell the peas. Cook the peas in the boiling water for 1 minute, then drain and immediately run under cold water.

When you're ready to serve, place a large frying pan over medium-high heat and add a glug of olive oil. Fry the beef cheeks in the pan for about 8 minutes, or until they are crisp. Remove from the pan and transfer to a large bowl. While they are still warm, use a potato peeler to slice the cucumbers lengthwise into ribbons and add to the beef cheeks in the bowl.

Add the peas and season with salt and pepper, then dress with the lemon juice and some olive oil. Grate in a tablespoon or so of the horseradish and give it all a gentle mix with your hands, letting the ingredients fall through your fingertips.

Gently lift the salad out of the bowl, again with your hands, and drop it onto a serving platter. A light touch is best here: the ingredients are delicate and you want them all to keep their elegant shapes. You also want to get some air through it. Scatter over any ingredients left behind in the bowl, along with the remaining dressing. Give the whole salad a final grating of horseradish and serve.

243

Pot-roasted Game Birds in Red Wine

There is something very satisfying and selfish about having a whole baby bird on your plate, with both legs and breast all to yourself. We used to serve this dish in mini pans; we would prepare the game birds in the pan, then take the entire pan to the table, lift the lid off, and leave the customer to serve themselves. We soon realized this was impractical because (a) the tables are tiny, as anyone who has been to Ducksoup knows, and (b) the customers were so excited to see what was inside the pot that when the lid came off they were almost burned by the plume of steam. Nowadays Tom has developed a much more sensible but equally theatrical way of serving them, in much smaller ceramic pots that we've had specially made, with lids. We still lift off the lids in front of the customers, revealing the birds with a "Ta da!" We call them our "Ta da" pots. We use Barbera wine in this recipe, but you can use any full-bodied Italian red wine here. Just choose one that you like drinking, so you can enjoy a well-deserved glass while you're cooking.

SERVES 4

4 partridges
Extra-virgin olive oil
6 oz [160 g] diced pancetta or bacon
1 onion, diced
2 carrots, cut into 1-in [2.5-cm] pieces
1 celery stalk, cut into 1-in [2.5-cm] pieces
1 leek, cut into 1-in [2.5-cm] pieces
1 head of garlic, cut in half horizontally
2 fresh bay leaves
Few thyme sprigs
1 tbsp tomato paste
2¼ cups [500 ml] Barbera or other good-quality red wine
2¼ cups [500 ml] chicken stock
1 cup [200 g] Castelluccio or Puy lentils
Handful of flat-leaf parsley
2 tbsp butter
Crusty bread, to serve
Salt and freshly ground black pepper

Preheat the oven to 400°F [200°C].

Place a large frying pan over medium-high heat while you rub the partridges with olive oil and season them with salt and pepper. →

Sear the birds in the pan, starting by searing one side for 2 minutes, then the other side for 2 minutes, and finally neck-side down for 2 minutes, or until golden brown. Depending on the size of your pan or how many you are cooking for, you may need to do this in batches. Once the birds are seared, remove and place them neck-side up in a large, lidded flameproof casserole that is big enough to hold all the birds and the sauce.

In the same frying pan, fry the pancetta or bacon pieces for about 2 minutes, then remove with a slotted spoon and add to the casserole. Add the vegetables, garlic, bay leaves, and thyme to the frying pan and cook for 8 to 10 minutes, or until caramelized, stirring every now and then.

Add the tomato paste and cook for 1 minute. Pour in the wine and allow to bubble and reduce slightly for 2 minutes. Add the stock and bring to a boil, then add to the birds in the casserole. Cover with a lid and roast for 15 minutes.

While the birds are roasting, bring a pan of salted water to a boil. Add the lentils and cook for 10 minutes, or until just cooked but still with a little bite; drain and put to one side.

When the birds are cooked, remove them from the casserole and allow to rest, covered loosely with foil, for 8 minutes. Put the casserole over high heat for 6 to 8 minutes, or until the sauce is reduced by half. Add the cooked lentils, tear in the parsley, and add the butter. Give it all a good stir and then put the birds back in with any juices they have released. Warm through for a couple of minutes and then serve directly from the pot with lots of crusty bread and, of course, a glass of Barbera.

Lamb Riblets & Za'atar

Prepare a big plate of these for a summer lunch—all you need to do is add the za'atar and let everyone descend. These are great if you're cooking a feast or having a few people over.

SERVES 4 (as part of a feast)
4½ lb [2 kg] lamb riblets
1 onion
1 head of garlic
Extra-virgin olive oil
2 fresh bay leaves
2 lemons, sliced
Few thyme sprigs
2¼ cups [500 ml] lamb stock
¼ cup [35 g] sesame seeds
2 tbsp sumac
2 tbsp dried oregano
Salt and freshly ground black pepper

Preheat the oven to 400°F [200°C] and heat a grill pan until smoking. Season the lamb riblets with salt and pepper and grill for 4 to 5 minutes on each side, or until they are nice and charred. You may need to do this in batches if your pan is small. Transfer the charred riblets to a high-sided roasting pan. Leaving the skin on, cut the onion in half and then cut each half into quarters through the root to keep the wedges together. Slice the head of garlic in half horizontally. Brush the onion and garlic with oil and season with salt and pepper. Cook in the grill pan until charred, and then add to the pan of riblets. Scatter the bay leaves, lemon slices, and thyme over all, and pour in the lamb stock.

Cover the pan tightly with foil and roast in the oven for 1 hour. After an hour, remove the foil from the pan and roast for a further 45 minutes, or until the riblets are nice and tender and the sauce has reduced slightly.

Meanwhile, make the za'atar by toasting the sesame seeds in a dry frying pan until golden, being careful not to burn them. Transfer to a bowl and combine with the sumac, oregano, and a good pinch of salt. When the riblets are cooked, serve straight from the roasting pan and sprinkle with a generous amount of your za'atar.

Spiced Lamb, Chickpeas & Labneh

This hearty lamb dish is served with partially blended chickpeas to give an almost mashlike consistency—perfect for mopping up the sauce and catching the meat that just slips off the bone—while the labneh adds a coolness to the spice. There is something intoxicating about slow-cooking lamb in this way: the heady aromatic spices and sweet dates fill the air and instantly transport you to bustling souks and fragrant kitchens in far-flung places.

SERVES 8

1 recipe labneh (see page 323)
1 bone-in lamb shoulder, about 6½ lb [3 kg]
¾ cup [200 ml] olive oil
2 tbsp cumin seeds
2 tbsp black mustard seeds
3½ oz [100 g] curry leaves (preferably fresh)
2 tbsp dried chile flakes
4 onions, diced
2 tbsp ground turmeric
6 garlic cloves, chopped
3½ oz [100 g] fresh ginger, peeled and chopped
13 oz [375 g] dates, chopped
2 lb [1 kg] tomatoes, chopped
3¾ cups [750 g] dried chickpeas, soaked overnight in cold water and drained
Salt

Prepare the labneh at least a day in advance and keep in the fridge until needed.

Preheat the oven to 325°F [160°C]. Place the lamb into a deep roasting pan and rub all over with salt. Put the lamb in the oven and slow-cook it for 4½ hours.

Meanwhile, warm the olive oil in a large pan over low heat and add the cumin seeds, black mustard seeds, curry leaves, and chile flakes. Simmer for 5 minutes, or until the seeds start to pop, being careful not to burn them. Add the onions and continue to cook over low heat until soft, 12 to 15 minutes.

Add the turmeric, garlic, ginger, dates, tomatoes, and 4½ cups [1 L] water and cook for a further 5 minutes.

Meanwhile, cook your chickpeas in double the amount of fresh water for 1 to 1½ hours or until just tender, skimming off the froth as they cook.

Remove about one-third of the chickpeas and place in a food processor with about ¾ cup [200 ml] of the cooking water. Process until smooth and then return to the pan with the whole chickpeas. Cook for a further 10 minutes—you're looking for a thick soup consistency.

When your lamb is cool enough to handle, remove from the bone in generous chunks and return it to the sauce in the roasting pan; keep warm.

To serve, spoon the chickpeas into bowls and spoon the lamb and sauce over them, making sure you keep can still see some of the chickpea mash underneath. Finish with a spoonful of labneh.

Roast Beef, Beets, Braised Lentils & Horseradish

An alternative to roast beef—particularly in the summer, when it makes a great lunch, and good as part of a sharing feast too.

SERVES 4
2 medium beets (or 1 large beet, halved)
Few thyme sprigs
2 tbsp red wine vinegar
Extra-virgin olive oil
1¼ cups [250 g] Puy lentils
1¾ lb [750 g] bavette steak
1 bunch of watercress
¼-in [5-mm] piece of fresh horseradish (or use good-quality horseradish from a jar)
Juice of 1 lemon
Salt and freshly ground pepper

Preheat the oven to 400°F [200°C].

To roast the beets, place them in a roasting pan with the thyme, red wine vinegar, a drizzle of olive oil, salt and pepper, and a drop of water. Cover tightly with foil and roast for 45 minutes.

Meanwhile, bring a large pan of water to a boil. Cook the lentils in the boiling water for 10 to 12 minutes, or until they are just tender but still have some bite (set your timer, because you don't want mushy lentils). Drain and spread out on a flat pan to cool.

Heat a grill pan until smoking while you rub the bavette with oil and season with salt and pepper. Grill for 4 to 5 minutes on each side— you're looking for good grill marks. Transfer to a roasting pan, add to the oven, and roast for 8 minutes. Remove and allow to rest on a pan for 10 minutes, loosely covered with foil.

Once the beets are cooked, peel them, keeping their cooking juices in the pan. Cut each beet in half at an angle (cut larger beets into quarters), then put them back into the pan and mix them into their juices.

Once the meat has rested, cut it across the grain at a slight angle, cutting it into nice chunks rather than straightforward slices. →

Divide the meat among four plates. Mix the beets with the lentils and a little of the beet cooking liquid. Stir just a couple of times because you don't want the lentils to go too red.

Spoon the lentils over the beef, making sure you can still see the meat underneath. Scatter a few watercress leaves over and then grate the horseradish over the top. Be as generous as you like, depending on how much heat you want. Squeeze a little lemon juice over the top, season with salt and pepper, and drizzle with some more olive oil.

Lamb Cooked in Milk & Wild Garlic

Cooking in milk is a well-worn tradition across many culinary cultures—it's said to tenderize the meat before you add other perhaps more astringent ingredients. Cook and serve straight from the roasting pan—it's an ideal feast dish if you're having people over—or cook it on the weekend and eat the leftovers through the week. If wild garlic isn't in season, then just use regular garlic (see below).

SERVES 6

1 bone-in lamb shoulder, about 6½ lb [3 kg]
Extra-virgin olive oil
4 onions, thinly sliced
2 heads of garlic, sliced in half horizontally (if wild garlic is not in season)
6 fresh bay leaves
Few thyme sprigs
8 cups [2 L] whole milk
2 lb [1 kg] fresh peas in the pod
1 lb [500 g] wild garlic leaves (if not using, 5 crushed heads of garlic)
Salt and freshly ground black pepper

Preheat the oven to 400°F [160°C]. Rub the lamb with olive oil and season well with salt and pepper. Place the lamb in a deep roasting pan and scatter the onions, garlic (if using), and herbs over it. Pour over the milk, cover tightly with foil, and roast for 4 hours, or until the meat is tender and falling off the bone.

Once cooked, remove the lamb shoulder from the roasting pan and set aside to cool slightly. Put the roasting pan on the stovetop over medium heat and add the peas. Using a wooden spatula, scrape the sides of the roasting pan to ensure that you catch the caramelized milk curds in the sauce, and cook for 2 minutes. Meanwhile, use a pair of tongs to remove the meat from the bone in large chunks and add to the sauce.

Season with salt and pepper. Just before serving, add the wild garlic leaves. It may seem like a lot, but, like spinach, the leaves will wilt down as soon as they hit the heat. Don't cook for longer than you need to, as the flavor of wild garlic is easily lost—you want to retain that fresh, aromatic garlic hit. Serve straight from the roasting pan with boiled new potatoes.

Duck Liver, Pancetta & Rosemary Ragu

This dish goes back to when we first opened, when Julian was head chef and Cinzia was our sous chef. She was a master in pasta making; Cinzia doesn't work with us anymore, but she came back recently to do a three-month stint, so Tom got her to train him in the art of pasta making. And now Tom's pasta is as good as Cinzia's... well, almost. Thanks, Cinzia.

You can make this a day ahead—it will taste even better once all the flavors have had more time to blend and strengthen.

SERVES 4

2 lb [1 kg] large, ripe tomatoes
Extra-virgin olive oil
6½ oz [180 g] pancetta, cut into lardons
1 onion, diced
Few rosemary sprigs, leaves chopped
4 bay leaves
4 garlic cloves, chopped
Pinch of dried chile flakes
14 oz [400 g] duck livers, cleaned and chopped
1 tbsp tomato paste
¾ cup [175 ml] red wine
11 oz [320 g] pappardelle (store-bought or homemade fresh pasta, see page 45)
Handful of flat-leaf parsley, coarsely chopped
Parmesan, for grating
Salt and freshly ground black pepper

First skin the tomatoes. Bring a large pan of salted water to a boil, large enough to hold the tomatoes. Using a sharp knife, score a little cross at the base of the tomatoes and cut out the "eye" of the tomato at the other end. Have a large bowl of ice water ready and, once your water is boiling, submerge the tomatoes for 15 seconds, then immediately plunge them into the ice water. You'll be able to peel off their skins almost immediately. Cut the tomatoes into quarters and remove the seeds, then coarsely chop and put to one side.

Place a large pan with a tight-fitting lid over medium-high heat. Add a little splash of oil and fry the pancetta for 5 minutes, or until golden brown. Remove from the pan with a slotted spoon, leaving the pancetta fat in the pan.

258

Add the onion to the pan and cook gently for 5 minutes, until soft but not colored. Add the rosemary, bay, garlic, and chile flakes and cook for a further 2 minutes. Once the onion and garlic soften, add the chopped duck livers, give everything a stir, and cook for 5 minutes, or until the livers are nice and colored on all sides.

Stir in the tomato paste and cook for 1 minute (cooking the tomato paste in hot oil like this, rather than just stirring it into liquid, brings out more of the flavor). Add the wine, bring to a boil, and reduce for 2 minutes, then add the chopped tomatoes and their juices. Reduce the heat, cover with the lid, and simmer for 45 minutes, stirring every now and then.

Meanwhile, bring a large pan of salted water to a boil for the pappardelle (allow about 15 minutes if you are using dried pasta, less if you are using fresh pasta). Cook the pasta according to the package instructions (or for 3 minutes if using fresh).

Once the ragu is cooked, remove from the heat and add the chopped parsley. Check the seasoning and grate some Parmesan straight into the pan.

Drain the pasta and add to the ragu. Give everything a good mix and then use a pair of tongs to pull the pasta through the sauce onto plates, then ladle over the ragu. Grate some more Parmesan over the top and drizzle with some extra-virgin olive oil.

Braised Rabbit Legs, White Wine, Tomatoes & Zucchini

We like cooking with rabbit in the restaurant; the meat is not too dissimilar to chicken but it has more flavor and is therefore more interesting to cook with. But if you can't get hold of rabbit or don't like the idea of eating it, you can easily replace it with chicken. This is ideal as a weekend lunch or dinner or, of course, as a weeknight supper if you're home early from work.

SERVES 4

4 rabbit legs (you can get these from a good butcher)
Extra-virgin olive oil
4 zucchini (we use round or yellow ones), cut into
    2-in [5-cm] chunks on the diagonal
1 white onion, sliced
4 garlic cloves, sliced
Few thyme sprigs
2 fresh bay leaves
1 cup [250 ml] white wine
4½ cups [1 L] chicken stock
6 plum tomatoes
Handful of mint and parsley leaves
Salt and freshly ground black pepper

Preheat the oven to 325°F [160°C].

Rub some olive oil into the rabbit legs and season with salt and pepper. Heat a large frying pan (big enough to hold the rabbit legs) over medium heat, add a little more oil to the pan, and then add the rabbit legs, rounded-side down (this will be the side that is face up on the plate). Cook for about 5 minutes, or until golden. Turn the rabbit legs over and cook for a further 5 minutes. Remove from the pan and place rounded-side up in a large roasting pan.

Add a tad more oil to the same frying pan and add the zucchini. Cook for 8 minutes, turning every now and then, until they are nice and golden. Remove from the pan and set aside.

Add a little more oil to the same pan, and cook the onion, garlic, and herbs over low heat until soft but not colored. This will take about

8 to 10 minutes. Pour in the wine and boil off the alcohol for about 2 minutes, then add the chicken stock. Coarsely chop the tomatoes (including the skin and seeds) and add to the pan. Bring to a boil and then carefully pour the stock over the rabbit legs. Cover the roasting pan with foil and place in the oven. After 1 hour, remove from the oven, take off the foil, and add the zucchini. Return to the oven and bake for a further 30 minutes, or until the rabbit legs are soft and tender and the meat is almost falling off the bone.

When the rabbit is cooked, tear over the mint and parsley leaves and gently stir in. Serve either on a large platter or divided among four plates. This goes nicely with new potatoes.

Like everything we do, these vibrant, sweet assemblies can be as simple as freshly picked seasonal fruit paired with crème fraîche, or tarts that will need baking. Our desserts are simple and delicious and there is no reason to save them for the weekend.

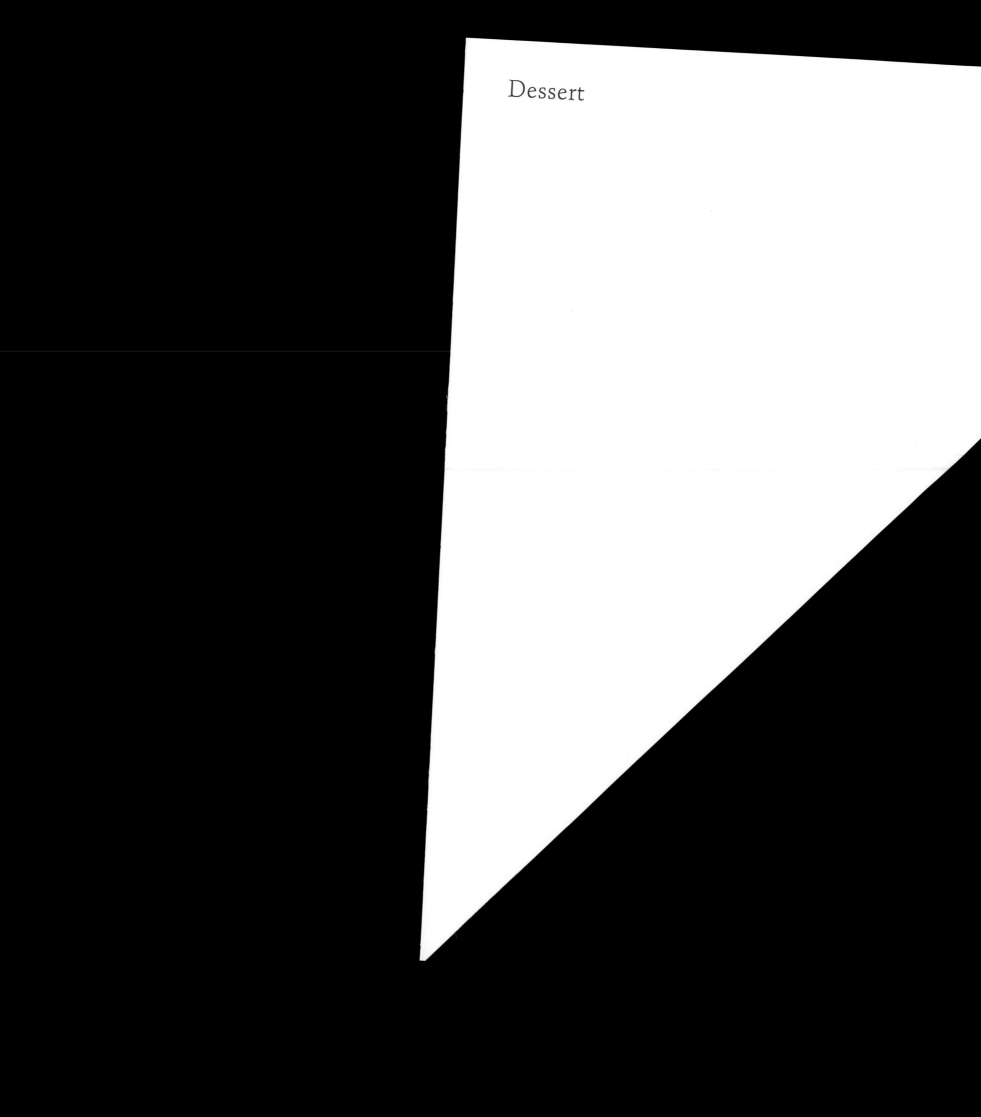

Dessert

Poached Rhubarb, Crème Fraîche Ice Cream & Hazelnut Crumb

We prefer to use as much rhubarb as possible at the beginning of the rhubarb season, because that's when it has a lovely bright pink color, which shows itself off in desserts such as this one. Of course, we continue using rhubarb in the summer, but the color is much less vibrant.

The ice cream mixture needs to chill in the fridge overnight, so prepare it at least a day in advance.

SERVES 4

For the ice cream
1 cup [250 ml] whole milk
½ cup [100 g] superfine sugar
6 egg yolks
Pinch of salt
1¾ cups [460 g] crème fraîche

For the rhubarb
1 cup [200 g] sugar
¾ cup [200 ml] water
2 lb [1 kg] early-forced rhubarb, cut into
   2-in [5-cm] lengths

For the crumble
½ cup [100 g] unsalted butter, diced
¾ cup [100 g] toasted hazelnuts,
   lightly crushed
½ cup [60 g] all-purpose flour
½ cup [60 g] rolled oats
⅓ cup [60 g] light brown sugar
Pinch of salt
1 tsp ground ginger

To make the ice cream, pour the milk into a pan and place over medium heat until it just comes to a boil.

Meanwhile, use a balloon whisk to whisk together the egg yolks and sugar until thick and pale; this will take about 8 minutes. Slowly pour in the hot milk, whisking all the time, until it is all combined.

Return the egg and milk mixture to a clean pan and add a pinch of salt. Cook the mixture over medium heat until it starts to thicken and coats the back of a spoon. When it has the right consistency, quickly pour it into a bowl to stop the mixture from sticking. Chill the mixture completely (in the fridge) and then stir in the crème fraîche. Return to the fridge to chill overnight.

The next day, pour the mixture into your ice cream maker and churn, following the manufacturer's instructions. Once churned, transfer to a suitable container and freeze for at least 3 hours before serving. →

If you don't have an ice cream maker, pour the mixture into a shallow container and place in the freezer; after an hour remove from the freezer and use a fork or whisk to break up the ice crystals. Return to the freezer and repeat this process every 30 minutes until the ice cream is smooth and creamy (you may need to do this four or five times). Freeze for 3 hours before serving.

Now you can make the crumble. Preheat the oven to 350°F [180°C]. Place all the crumble ingredients into a large bowl and use the tips of your fingers to rub together until the mixture resembles bread crumbs. Spread out onto a large baking pan and bake for 10 to 15 minutes, or until the crumble is golden brown. Remove from the oven and allow to cool while you poach the rhubarb.

Heat the superfine sugar and water in a pan until simmering, stirring as you go to dissolve the sugar. Cook the rhubarb pieces in batches in the sugar syrup, poaching them for about 1 minute. Remove with a slotted spoon and arrange flat on a baking pan. Once you've poached all the rhubarb, let the sugar syrup cool down and then pour it over the rhubarb. Allow to sit for about 1 hour for the flavors to combine.

To serve, spoon the rhubarb and the juices into bowls and top with scoops of the ice cream. Finish with a good sprinkling of the crumble over the top.

Milk Pudding & Red Wine Poached Pears

Milk puddings suit the way we cook: light and clean, they are a nice note on which to end dinner. They can take on many different flavors and ingredients, from bergamot and rose water to honeycomb and nuts, so you can make them suit whatever style of food you are cooking. We use disposable ⅔-cup [150-ml] foil molds, which you can buy from cookware shops or online, but you can also use ramekins.

SERVES 4

1½ cups [375 ml] whole milk
½ cup [125 ml] heavy cream
¾ cup [100 g] confectioners' sugar
3½ sheets gelatin
2 Comice pears (or any pears in season)
1 lemon
2¼ cups [500 ml] red wine
1 fresh bay leaf
¼ cup [50 g] granulated sugar
2 cardamom pods, lightly crushed
4 black peppercorns

Pour the milk, cream, and confectioners' sugar into a pan and warm together over medium heat for 5 minutes. Remove from the heat. Meanwhile, put the gelatin in a bowl of cold water and leave for 5 minutes to soften or "bloom." Then squeeze out the excess water and whisk the gelatin into the hot milk. Pour this mixture into your molds and cool before placing in the fridge to set for at least 8 hours or overnight.

Make the poached pears. Peel, quarter, and core the pears, then cut each quarter in half at a slight 45-degree angle. Set aside. Use a vegetable peeler to pare off the lemon rind in strips and add to a pan with the red wine, bay leaf, granulated sugar, and spices. Place over low heat and bring to a simmer. Add the pears, cover with a lid, and simmer for about 5 minutes, or until just soft, stirring the pears halfway through. Take off the heat and allow to cool, stirring every now and then so all the pears get a good soaking in the wine.

When you are ready to serve, boil a small pan of water and dip each mold in for 2 seconds, then turn them out onto individual plates. Add a spoonful of the poached pear, along with a little poaching liquid.

Apple, Prune & Hazelnut Galette

A galette doesn't rely as much on the consistency of oven heat as a tart does, where you want the heat to be perfectly even all over. Here the pastry needs to be perfect, as does the quality of the fruit you are using. We've made galettes with just about every fruit going, from pears and strawberries to plums and rhubarb, so do experiment with whatever fruits you have and see what happens.

SERVES 8–12

For the pastry
2⅔ cups [375 g] all-purpose flour
⅓ cup [50 g] cornstarch
1 cup [200 g] unsalted butter, chilled
    and cut into ⅜-in [1-cm] dice
1 cup [100 g] sugar
¼ cup [60 g] crème fraîche
Juice of ½ lemon
Pinch of salt
Beaten egg, to glaze

For the filling
4 Braeburn apples (or any apple in season)
2 tbsp dark brown sugar, plus extra
    for sprinkling
Juice of ½ lemon
1¼ cups [200 g] pitted prunes
Handful of toasted hazelnuts
Crème fraîche or ice cream, to serve
    (optional)

First make the pastry. Tip the flour and cornstarch into a food processor and add the diced butter. Pulse until you have a coarse crumb texture—you want to have small clumps of butter visible throughout the flour.

Add the remaining pastry ingredients (except the beaten egg) and pulse briefly to combine, adding a dash of cold water if needed to bring it together into a dough. Don't overwork the dough, as you don't want all the butter fully combined. Tip out onto a work surface, pat into a ball, and wrap in plastic wrap. Chill in the fridge for a couple of hours.

Meanwhile, make the filling. Quarter your apples and remove the cores. Use a mandoline slicer to thinly slice the apples and put them in a mixing bowl. Add the sugar, lemon juice, prunes, and hazelnuts and give it a good mix with your hands. Leave to macerate at room temperature until needed.

Once your pastry is chilled, preheat the oven to 350°F [180°C]. →

Lay a large sheet of parchment paper on a work surface and dust with flour. Place the pastry on the parchment and, with a floured rolling pin, roll the pastry out to a circle approximately 14 to 16 in [35 to 40 cm] in diameter and ⅛ in [3 mm] thick. The pastry will be quite soft, so take care.

Tip the filling along with the juices onto the pastry and spread it out, leaving a 2-in [5-cm] border all around. Fold the border over the fruit filling—this process doesn't need to be too neat, and if the pastry tears, just pinch it back together. Remember, this is a rustic galette; it wouldn't sit right in a French patisserie, but that's the point.

Once you've folded in the edges, brush them with beaten egg and sprinkle with a little brown sugar. Slide the galette, still on the parchment paper, onto a baking sheet and bake for 30 to 35 minutes, or until the pastry is golden brown and the filling is cooked. Serve hot, with crème fraîche or ice cream.

Black Figs & Toasted Sesame Ice Cream

Ice cream is Tom's Achilles' heel (or his vice). Rory loves it so much that he used to throw ice cream parties. The two are quite competitive when it comes to making ice cream, which is a good thing, as it means we're always making it at the restaurant. A well-made ice cream using good ingredients is the stuff that dreams are made of. This toasted sesame seed ice cream is really special and works very well with summer-ripe figs.

SERVES 4
For the ice cream
1¼ cups [300 ml] milk
1¼ cups [300 ml] whipping cream
½ cup [100 g] superfine sugar
6 egg yolks
Pinch of salt
⅓ cup [40 g] sesame seeds

1 lb [500 g] ripe black figs
½ cup [100 g] superfine sugar

To make the ice cream, heat the milk and cream together over medium heat until it starts to bubble around the edges, then remove the pan from the heat.

Using a balloon whisk, whisk the sugar and egg yolks together with a pinch of salt until thick and frothy; this will take about 8 minutes. Slowly pour the hot milk and cream into the egg mixture, whisking as you go. Once everything is mixed together, pour the mixture into a clean pan and place over medium heat. Cook the custard for about 5 minutes, stirring continuously, until it starts to thicken. As soon as it's thick enough to coat the back of a spoon, pour the mixture into a container, allow to cool, and then put into the fridge.

Meanwhile, toast the sesame seeds in a dry frying pan for about 2 minutes, shaking the pan to ensure they turn an even golden color. Once the custard is completely cool, whisk in the toasted sesame seeds, reserving a few to sprinkle over just before serving. Pour the mixture into your ice cream maker and churn, following the manufacturer's instructions. →

Once churned, transfer to a suitable container and freeze for at least 3 hours before serving. If you don't have an ice cream maker, pour the mixture into a shallow container and place in the freezer; after an hour remove from the freezer and use a fork or whisk to break up the ice crystals. Return to the freezer and repeat this process every 30 minutes until the ice cream is smooth and creamy (you may need to do this four or five times).

While your ice cream is freezing, make the fig compote by tearing the figs into quarters into a bowl. Add the sugar, give them a good stir, and leave to macerate for 2 hours. After 2 hours, pour the macerated figs and all the sugar and juices into a pan and place over low heat. Gently simmer for 8 to 10 minutes, or until the sugar has dissolved (take care not to let the sugar burn).

Once your fig compote is ready, spoon into bowls and top with a couple of scoops of ice cream. Sprinkle a few more toasted sesame seeds over the top, if you like.

Bergamot Milk Pudding
& Earl Grey Tea-soaked Prunes

When we first opened Ducksoup, Nick Strangeway would come by with a backpack full of ingredients for his latest cocktail experiments. One day he came in apparently wearing a new scent. When asked what it was, he pulled two bergamots from his bag. From that day we've used bergamot a lot in our cooking, and our drinks. Bergamot is a beautiful citrus but is potent, so go easy. Here we use Agen prunes because of their good balance of sugar and acidity, plus their strong skins mean they dry well, although you can use any prunes. You will need four ⅔-cup [150-ml] molds or ramekins.

SERVES 4

1½ cups [375 ml] whole milk
½ cup [125 ml] heavy cream
Zest and juice of 1 bergamot
¾ cup [100 g] confectioners' sugar
2 sheets of leaf gelatin
1½ cups [250 g] pitted prunes (we use Agen)
1 tsp honey
2 Earl Grey tea bags

Put the milk, cream, bergamot zest, and confectioners' sugar into a pan and warm over low heat for about 8 minutes. Leave for 15 minutes to infuse. Meanwhile, put the gelatin in a bowl of cold water and leave for 5 minutes to soften or "bloom." Once softened, squeeze out the excess water and whisk the gelatin into the hot milk.

Allow the mixture to cool at room temperature, and then slowly add the bergamot juice. Pass the mixture through a sieve to get rid of the bergamot zest and pour it into your molds. Place in the fridge to set for 8 hours or overnight.

Put the prunes in a large bowl. Pour 2¼ cups [500ml] boiling water (from a kettle) into a jug and add the honey; stir to dissolve. Add the tea bags and brew for 10 minutes, then strain and pour over your prunes. Allow the prunes to marinate in the tea for as long as it takes the milk puddings to set. When you're ready to serve, have a small pan of boiling water at the ready. Dip each mold into the hot water for no more than 2 seconds, then turn each out onto a plate. Arrange a few prunes around the puddings and spoon the juice over them.

Orange Blossom & Milk Pudding, Pistachios & Honeycomb

Bergamot, orange blossom, rose water—these are all scents that we really enjoy cooking with. The intoxicating smell of a tiny drop of orange blossom water can transport you to a million different places. It's traditionally used in Middle Eastern cooking, mainly in desserts, but has also found its way to Europe and is used to flavor madeleines. In Morocco it is also used as a cleanser to wash your hands before you enter a house or take tea—how lovely! Needless to say, this is a Middle Eastern–inspired pudding.

You will need four ⅔-cup [150-ml] molds or ramekins.

SERVES 4
1½ cups [375 ml] whole milk
½ cup [125 ml] heavy cream
¾ cup [100 g] confectioners' sugar
3½ sheets leaf gelatin
2 tbsp orange blossom water
¼ cup [20 g] honeycomb
⅓ cup [40 g] pistachios, warmed in a dry frying pan and lightly crushed

Pour the milk, cream, and confectioners' sugar into a pan and warm together over medium heat for 5 minutes. Remove from the heat.

Meanwhile, put the gelatin in a bowl of cold water and leave for 5 minutes to soften or "bloom." Once softened, squeeze out the excess water and whisk the gelatin into the hot milk, then add the orange blossom water. Pour this mixture into your molds and allow to cool before placing in the fridge to set for at least 8 hours or overnight.

When you are ready to serve, have a small pan of boiling water at the ready. Dip each mold into the hot water for no longer than 2 seconds, and then turn each pudding out onto a plate. Add a spoonful of honeycomb on the side and sprinkle the crushed pistachios over the top.

On Music
Rory McCoy

Music is a big part of what we do at Ducksoup. The day we opened the doors we had the vinyl on. Things wouldn't be the same without it. We're strong believers in vinyl—playlists just feel soulless. We started with just a handful of records but now have a collection of about 250.

Music goes hand in hand with cooking and feeding friends—it creates atmosphere, brings harmony to a room, or just helps jolly you along as you cook. We've had memorable conversations with customers about music and their connection to it. For over 30 years my uncle John had an incredible music venue called the Kirklevington Country Club, which attracted the greatest musicians from the 1960s onward, so music has always been part of my life. Having customers and staff who love music has spurred us on, and influenced what we buy.

Here are our top five music styles and some of our favorite albums to cook and eat to.

1. Slide guitar

Ry Cooder: *Bop till You Drop*, 1979, and *Chicken Skin Music*, 1976
I was introduced to Ry Cooder and JJ Cale by my uncle Christie. It was always played in

my family's restaurant. Christie loved Chris Rea's slide guitar, and I did too, especially the track "No Work Today." Ry's sound has a similar distinct style that cuts through you. His American roots music sees him collaborate with different music styles and attracts the most celebrated, and not always famous, artists in that genre. *Bop till You Drop* is a gem. Its slide and deep-voiced male singers are perfect for slow weekend-style cooking. *Chicken Skin Music* is an eclectic mix of American folk, banjos, and clunky, half-drunk New Orleans jazz band members. It's a great daytime soundtrack.

2. Great piano songwriters

Elton John: *Tumbleweed Connection*, 1970, and *17-11-70*, 1971
People often cringe when I say, "Let's put on Elton John." Elton gets a bad rap for overplayed or rotten songs, and there have certainly been some, but he and Bernie Taupin have together also written some of the best songs ever. Elton's first few albums were masterpieces of melody and lyrics, and *Tumbleweed Connection* is just that, beautifully evoking the American Western frontier. Bought for me by my uncle Kevin when I was 14, it changed my musical world, and it was one of the first 10 vinyls we bought for Ducksoup. You can play the whole album through, for lunch and mellow evenings. Whereas the rock 'n' roll Elton, who comes

along in the live album *17-11-70*, is ideal for when you are all standing and socializing.

Van Morrison: *Saint Dominic's Preview*, 1972
When I want to up the ante, I play track 1, "Jackie Wilson Said." Although a classic in its time, over the decades it has now become just one of many greats. It's good to have the albums of the major artists that aren't so well known or, even better, are forgotten. The song kicks in within seconds and it's infectious, foot-tapping music.

3. Reggae

Toots & the Maytals: *Funky Kingston*, 1975 pressing
Jimmy Cliff: *The Harder They Come*, 1972
Reggae: it's not important, it's essential. And these are classics. If you don't have "Funky Kingston" by Toots & the Maytals or "Pressure Drop" by Jimmy Cliff at your fingertips, it can hurt. Pouring with energy, these are ones to cook to with a glass of wine in your hand. They will really get you in the mood and pick you up before your guests arrive.

4. Blues

B.B. King: *Take It Home*, 1979, and *Live at the Regal*, 1965
Thanks to my father's piano playing, blues is the backbone of my life and our collection at

Ducksoup. We play John Mayall, Muddy Waters, Professor Longhair, Long John Baldry, or Barbara Lynn daily, but I chose B.B. King here out of all the other blues musicians because his sound has the hook: his guitar picking, his guitar that sings the melody. It resonates with your internal core and enhances the moment, which, hopefully, coincides with a glass of rich red wine.

5. Folk, Rock, and Country

Loudon Wainwright III: *Attempted Mustache*, 1973
The LP cover is a close-up of his own mustache and the opening track, "The Swimming Song," can never be overplayed. Loudon has a youthful folk sound—it's fun in spite of the brutal honesty of his lyrics, which creates a beauty, deep and yet cruel to those he loves. To be played on repeat while entertaining outside in hot weather.

Neil Young: *After the Gold Rush*, 1970
Our collective favorite. If you want a 10-minute, one-string guitar solo before dessert, try track 4, "Southern Man," to be played with drunk and well-fed friends. You can all sing along and get lost in deep conversation about when you first heard the album.

Peaches, Raspberries & Crème Fraîche

Ripe peaches, strawberries, raspberries, apricots, and a wealth of other summer fruits are just ideal for tearing apart, throwing into a bowl, adding a little sugar, and letting them macerate in their own juices. Add a dollop of crème fraîche or ice cream. Divine. We think there is something extra special about the pairing of peaches and raspberries.

SERVES 4
4 ripe peaches
2 pints of raspberries, about 9 oz [250 g] in total
1 tbsp turbinado or other coarse sugar
¾ cup [200 g] crème fraîche
Dessert wine (optional)

Cut the peaches in half, cutting around the pit, and then twist each half in opposite directions to expose the pit. Remove the pits (do this over a bowl so you collect the juices), then gently tear each half in half again and drop into the bowl.

Add the raspberries and sugar and give everything a good toss to combine. Leave to macerate in the sugar and juices for 5 minutes.

Lay the fruit out on a serving platter and top with generous dollops of crème fraîche. Enjoy with a cheeky glass of dessert wine, such as Sauternes, or even pour one over the top of the fruits.

Rice Pudding & Rose Water Jelly

This dessert came about when we were going through one of our more homey phases, while the addition of rose water jelly is a result of Tom's time making jams and preserves at Rawduck. The dish reminds us of childhood desserts, when your granny would add a spoonful of jam to your semolina, and so it suddenly fit even more perfectly into our quest for more nostalgic puddings.

SERVES 4

For the rice pudding
6 tbsp [80 g] butter
1 cup [180 g] risotto rice
⅓ cup [80 g] granulated sugar
5 cups [1.2 L] whole organic milk
½ cup [120 ml] heavy cream
Pinch of salt

For the rose water jelly
1 lemon
2 lb [1 kg] quinces
About 3¾ cups [750 g] superfine sugar
2 tbsp rose water

Start by making the jelly—you'll need to do this at least a day in advance. Pare the rind off the lemon in strips and then squeeze the juice. Add both rind and juice to a medium pan with about 4 cups [1 L] water. Use a vegetable peeler to peel the quinces, then remove the cores, cut into quarters, and add to the pan of water. Make sure the quince is fully immersed in the water. Place over medium heat and simmer for about 15 minutes, or until soft.

Once soft, lightly mash the quince in the pan and then strain through a sieve lined with a double layer of muslin into a bowl. This will take some time, so ideally leave it overnight—find a good spot where it can do its thing, somewhere cool. You want to extract as much juice as possible, but don't be tempted to rush it by squeezing the juice through or you will end up with cloudy jelly.

The following day (or at least 8 hours later), pour your strained juice into a measuring cup (keep your pulp to make quince cheese—see opposite). As a guideline, you will need 3¾ cups [750 g] superfine sugar for every 4½ cups [1 L] juice. To work this out, simply divide the total liquid you have by 100, then multiply by 75 to get the quantity of sugar you need.

Combine your quince juice and superfine sugar in a heavy-bottomed pan and slowly bring to a boil, stirring to dissolve the sugar as it warms.

You've now got the beginnings of jelly. At this point you want to keep it on a rapid boil until it reaches 221°F [104.9°C] on a candy thermometer. If you don't have a candy thermometer, you can do the plate test: put a couple of small plates in the freezer for about 15 minutes. Once the jelly has thickened, pour a small amount on to the plate and count to 10. If you can run your finger through the jelly to divide it into two, it means you have jelly. It's a good idea to keep a couple of plates in the freezer in case you need to repeat the test.

When your jelly has passed the test, take it off the heat and stir in the rose water. Decant into a sterilized canning jar (see page 43) and allow to cool.

To make the rice pudding, melt the butter in a large pan over medium heat. When it starts foaming, add the rice and fry for a couple of minutes. Add the granulated sugar and milk and cook slowly for 1 hour, stirring every so often, until the rice is cooked and thickened. Finish by stirring in the heavy cream and a pinch of salt.

To serve, divide the rice pudding among four bowls (or pour into one large bowl) and place the jar of rose water jelly in the middle of the table for everyone to help themselves—it looks so much nicer.

The By-product: Quince Cheese

Remove the lemon rind from the quince pulp and then weigh the pulp. As in the jelly, you will need 3¾ cups [750 g] sugar for every 2 lb [1 kg] pulp, so use the same calculation described earlier to work out how much sugar you need. Put both the pulp and sugar in a food processor or blender and blend until smooth. Pour the mixture into a pan and place over medium heat, stirring to dissolve the sugar. Once dissolved, reduce the heat to a low simmer and cook until you can run a wooden spoon through the mixture, dividing the mixture and creating a prominent line on the bottom of the pan (think Moses parting the Red Sea). You'll need to stir continuously to prevent the mixture separating. Line a shallow plastic container or baking dish with plastic wrap. Once the mixture is ready, pour it into the container and spread evenly. Leave to cool for 2 hours before placing in the fridge to fully set—this will take about 12 hours. You now have quince cheese—cut into slices and serve with cheese. It will keep in the fridge for a few weeks.

Almond & Strawberry Tart

This is a simple almond and strawberry tart—nothing out of the ordinary—but when the ingredients are impeccable and you get the almond base sticky and rich-tasting the way fresh almonds do (as though soaked in amaretto) and then top with giant ripe and juicy strawberries and a sprinkling of confectioners' sugar, it suddenly becomes something a lot less ordinary. It's now a firm Ducksoup summer favorite and will go down so well if you're feeding a few.

SERVES 8–12

For the pastry

2¼ cups [300 g] all-purpose flour, plus extra for dusting
½ cup [60 g] confectioners' sugar
⅔ cup [150 g] unsalted butter, chilled and cut into small dice, plus extra for greasing
1 egg, beaten

For the filling

1 cup [250 g] butter, at room temperature
1¼ cups [250 g] granulated sugar
3 eggs
⅓ cup [50 g] all-purpose flour
2 cups [240 g] almond meal
1 to 2 tbsp good-quality strawberry jam
Large pint of strawberries
Handful of toasted sliced almonds
Confectioners' sugar, for dusting (optional)

First make the pastry. Put the flour and confectioners' sugar into a food processor and pulse briefly to combine. Add the butter and pulse again until the butter is incorporated (you can also do this by hand using a large bowl and a round-bladed knife). Don't overwork the pastry; otherwise, it will shrink when you bake it. It's fine to leave a few lumps of butter here and there, as it will make for a better pastry. Finally, add the egg to bring everything together. If the mixture is still a little dry, add a splash of ice water.

Shape the pastry into a disk about 1 in [3 cm] thick (this will make it easier to roll out). Wrap in plastic wrap and chill in the fridge for at least 1 hour.

To make the filling, first cream together the butter and granulated sugar in a food processor or stand mixer, until the butter and sugar are combined and the mixture is pale and fluffy. You can do this by hand too but it will take a little longer. Keep mixing on medium-low speed and add the eggs one at a time, mixing well after each addition. If you are mixing by hand, beat the eggs into the butter quickly so that the mixture doesn't curdle. →

Once all your eggs are combined, add the flour and almond meal and mix well. Place the mixture in the fridge to chill while you roll out the pastry.

Lightly grease a 12-in [30-cm] loose-bottomed tart pan with a nugget of soft butter and a dusting of flour; this will prevent the tart from sticking. Dust your work surface and rolling pin with flour and start to roll the pastry away from you. Turn it by 45 degrees and roll away from you again. Continue in this way until the pastry is about ¼ in [5 mm] thick and about 3 in [8 cm] larger in diameter than your tart pan.

Roll the pastry onto your rolling pin, lift it up, and then carefully drape it over the tart pan. Using your fingers, gently ease the pastry into the corners and sides of the pan, ready for the filling. Chill the pastry-lined pan in the fridge for 25 minutes—the colder the butter in the pastry, the less likely it is to melt, causing the pastry to crack. You can speed this process up by putting it in the freezer. Preheat the oven to 350°F [180°C].

When you are ready to bake the tart, remove the filling and the pastry-lined pan from the fridge and line the pastry with parchment paper. Fill with dried beans and blind-bake for 20 minutes, or until the sides start to turn golden. Remove the paper and beans and return to the oven for a further 5 minutes to cook the base. If any cracks form in the pastry, beat an egg and simply brush it over the pastry base before returning it to the oven for 5 minutes.

Remove the baked pastry shell from the oven and reduce the temperature to 325°F [160°C]. Spread a layer of strawberry jam over the base, followed by the almond filling, spreading it out to fill the shell. Return to the oven for 20 to 25 minutes, or until the top is golden and it doesn't wobble if you give it a little shake. Remove from the oven and allow to cool before separating it from the pan.

To finish, scatter the whole strawberries over the top of the tart (cut any large strawberries in half). Sprinkle the sliced almonds over the top, and finally dust with a little confectioners' sugar.

Dark Chocolate Mousse, Sour Cherries & Pistachios

Lydia Hix and I were having a bit of a raw moment and came across a raw chocolate bar with sour cherries in it. We took this idea and tried experimenting at home, making raw chocolate with various different fruits and nuts. From this Tom produced this silky, dark chocolate mousse with sour cherries and pistachios. We like to serve this loose rather than set in molds, just spooned onto plates with the cherries and pistachios scattered over the top.

SERVES 6–8
9 oz [250 g] dark chocolate, minimum 70% cocoa solids
¼ cup [50 g] unsalted butter, softened
6 egg yolks
10 egg whites
3 tbsp superfine sugar
Handful of dried sour cherries
Handful of shelled pistachios

Break the chocolate into pieces and place with the butter in a heatproof bowl set over a pan over just simmering water. Make sure the base of the bowl doesn't touch the water; otherwise, the chocolate will scald and burn. When the chocolate and butter are all melted, remove from the heat.

Meanwhile, whisk the egg yolks in a separate bowl until thick and the mixture leaves a "ribbon" trail when the whisk is lifted out of the bowl. In another clean bowl, using a handheld electric mixer, whisk the egg whites until soft peaks form. Start slowly and then gradually build up speed as you slowly add the sugar. Whisk until the sugar is all combined.

Add the egg yolks to the egg whites and gently fold in, then fold a quarter of the egg mixture into the melted chocolate; the mixture will be a little stiff. At this point gently fold the chocolate into the rest of the egg mixture, ensuring you fold in as much air in as possible.

Pour into a large bowl and chill in the fridge for 1 hour. When you are ready to serve, spoon onto individual plates and scatter the cherries and pistachios over the top.

Walnut, Rum & Honey Tart

This is one of our "go-to" classic tarts. With nuts and booze in it, there's not much to dislike. A great seasonal party piece.

SERVES 8–12

For the pastry
2¼ cups [300 g] all-purpose flour, plus
    extra for dusting
½ cup [60 g] confectioners' sugar
⅔ cup [150 g] unsalted butter, chilled and
    cut into ⅜-in [1-cm] dice, plus extra
    for greasing
1 egg

For the filling
3⅓ cups [400 g] walnut halves
⅓ cup [75 g] dark brown sugar
⅔ cup [130 g] unsalted butter, chilled and
    cut into ⅜-in [1-cm] dice
½ cup [175 g] clear honey
8 egg yolks
½ cup [125 ml] heavy cream
⅓ cup [75 ml] dark rum

Clotted cream, to serve

First make the sweet pastry. Put the flour and confectioners' sugar into a food processor and pulse briefly to combine. Add the butter and pulse again until the butter is incorporated (you can also do this by hand, using a large bowl and a round-bladed knife). Don't overwork the pastry; otherwise it will shrink when you bake it. Finally, add the egg to bring everything together. If the mixture is still a little dry, add a splash of ice-cold water.

Shape the pastry into a round disk about 1 in [3 cm] thick (this will make it easier to roll out). Wrap in plastic wrap and chill in the fridge for a couple of hours until needed (you can make this the day before if you prefer).

To make the filling, use your hands to crush the walnuts into a large bowl, add the rest of the ingredients, and mix well. Don't worry if your butter is still in rough lumps.

Lightly grease a 12-in [30-cm] loose-bottomed tart pan with a nugget of soft butter and a dusting of flour; this will prevent the tart from sticking. Dust your work surface and rolling pin with flour and start to roll the pastry away from you. Turn it by 45 degrees and roll away from you again. Continue in this way until the pastry is about ¼ in [5 mm] thick and about 3 in [8 cm] larger in diameter than your tart pan.

Roll the pastry onto your rolling pin, lift it up, and then carefully drape it over the tart pan. Using your fingers, gently ease the pastry into the corners and sides of the pan, ready for the filling. Chill the pastry-lined pan in the fridge for 25 minutes—the colder the butter in the pastry, the less likely it is to melt, causing the pastry to crack. You can speed this process up by putting it in the freezer. Preheat the oven to 350°F [180°C].

When you are ready to bake the tart, remove the filling and the pastry-lined pan from the fridge and line the pastry with parchment paper. Fill with dried beans and blind-bake for 20 minutes, or until the sides start to turn golden. Remove the paper and beans and return to the oven for a further 5 minutes to cook the base. If any cracks form in the pastry, beat an egg and simply brush it over the pastry base before returning it to the oven for 5 minutes.

Remove the baked pastry shell from the oven and pour in the filling, making sure the walnuts are evenly spread across the tart. Bake for 15 to 20 minutes, or until the filling is set and the walnuts are toasted.

Allow the tart to cool slightly before separating it from the pan. Serve with a generous dollop of clotted cream.

Brillat-Savarin Cheesecake 3 Ways

Brillat-Savarin is a soft cream cheese produced in the Île-de-France region and named after the famous French gastronome Jean Anthelme Brillat-Savarin. It has a fat content of at least 75 percent, which is achieved by adding cream to whole milk. This makes it a perfect dessert cheese and, it's what we use to make our "deconstructed" cheesecake, although you could also use Philadelphia cream cheese—it will still taste delicious. On the following pages we give three of our favorite ways of serving it, using different seasonal ingredients.

SERVES 4 GENEROUSLY

For the crumb
3 tbsp unsalted butter
10 graham crackers or digestive biscuits

For the cheesecake mix
7 oz [200 g] Brillat-Savarin
⅓ cup [80 g] crème fraîche
½ cup [240 g] Greek yogurt
¾ cup [200 g] mascarpone
Few drops of lemon juice

Melt the butter in a small pan over a low heat. While it is melting, crush the graham crackers (or biscuits) in a large bowl using the end of a rolling pin. When the butter has melted, stir it into your crumbs and place in the fridge to chill.

Place all your ingredients for the cheesecake mix into a large bowl and gently combine using a large spoon. Don't overmix, as you want to have little nuggets of cheese running through the mix. The idea is that it's roughly folded through so that you get the different textures.

Assemble and serve as suggested on the following pages.

1. Strawberries & Almonds

14 oz [400 g] strawberries
3 tbsp sugar
Few drops of lemon juice
Handful of toasted sliced almonds

Hull the strawberries and mix in a bowl with the sugar and lemon juice. Leave to macerate for 10 to 15 minutes for the juices to draw out and make a little syrup.

Make the crumb as on page 299, but crush in the toasted almonds along with the crackers, and make the cheesecake mix.

To serve, spoon the crumb (about a tablespoon per person) into a bowl or on a plate, then place a large spoon of your cheesecake mix over the top. Finish with a generous spoon of the macerated strawberries.

2. Blackberries & Hazelnuts

14 oz [400 g] blackberries
2 tbsp brown sugar
Splash of apple juice
Handful of toasted hazelnuts

Mix the blackberries, sugar, and apple juice together and leave to macerate for 10 to 15 minutes.

Make the crumb as on page 299, but crush in the toasted hazelnuts along with the crackers, and make the cheesecake mix.

To serve, spoon the crumb (about a tablespoon per person) into a bowl or on a plate, then place a large spoon of your cheesecake mix over the top. Finish with a generous spoon of the macerated blackberries.

3. Blood Orange Curd

The blood orange curd will keep for up to 2 weeks in an airtight container in the fridge, so make a big batch and have it for your breakfast with sourdough or yogurt.

Zest and juice of 5 blood oranges
1 cup [225 g] unsalted butter, cut into ⅜-in [1-cm] dice
1¼ cups [250 g] sugar
6 eggs, plus 2 egg yolks

Make the crumb and cheesecake mix as on page 299. Bring to a gentle simmer a large pan of water, one over which your heatproof bowl will sit comfortably.

Put the blood orange zest and juice into a heatproof bowl and add the diced butter, along with the sugar, eggs, and egg yolks.

Place the bowl over the pan of boiling water, making sure that the base of the bowl does not touch the water; otherwise, the mixture will heat too quickly and you'll end up with scrambled blood orange. Let everything slowly cook together, giving it a gentle whisk as it cooks. After about 15 minutes the mixture will start to thicken as the eggs cook. Once the mixture is the consistency of heavy cream, pour through a fine-mesh sieve into a clean container. Place in the fridge to chill until you're ready to serve.

To serve, spoon the crumb (about a tablespoon per person) into a bowl or on a plate, then place a large spoon of your cheesecake mix over the top. Finish with a generous spoon of the curd and a final sprinkle of crumb.

Roast Pears, Mascarpone Cream & Walnut Brittle

Pears are one of our favorite fruits—they lend themselves to both savory winter salads and sweet desserts. Make more brittle than you need and munch on it throughout the week or, of course, keep it for the following weekend when you might need to eat this dessert again.

SERVES 4

1⅔ cups [200 g] walnut halves
2 cups [400 g] granulated sugar
Pinch of salt
½ cup [125 ml] heavy cream
1 cup [250 g] mascarpone
1 tbsp confectioners' sugar
2 large Comice pears (or any pears in season)
Walnut oil

First make the walnut brittle. Line a baking pan with parchment paper, and toast the walnuts in a dry frying pan over medium heat for 5 minutes. Don't overcook them or they will go bitter. Tip them out onto a cutting board and crush them a little with a rolling pin, then spread them out on the lined baking pan.

Heat the granulated sugar and salt in a heavy-bottomed pan over medium-high heat. Give the pan a gentle shake as the sugar starts to caramelize to prevent it from coloring too much around the outside edges. Watch the caramel as it cooks, as you don't want it to burn—you may need to reduce the heat. Keep shaking the pan to move the liquid around, and then, as soon as the sugar turns a golden color, after 10 to 12 minutes, pour it over the walnuts. Set aside to cool.

When the brittle is cool and hard, peel it off the parchment paper and break it into a sturdy bowl. Use the end of a rolling pin to smash up the brittle until it looks like coarse bread crumbs.

To make the mascarpone cream, gently whisk the cream in a bowl until it forms soft peaks—this will only take a couple of minutes—then use a spatula to stir in the mascarpone and confectioners' sugar.

Prepare the pears by cutting them in half lengthwise and then cutting each half into three wedges, cutting out the core. Heat a frying pan over medium-high heat and add a dash of oil. Cook the pears, cut-side down, for 3 minutes, or until they turn golden brown; turn and cook the other side for 3 minutes more.

To serve, arrange three pear wedges on each plate, top with a generous dollop of mascarpone cream, and scatter the walnut brittle over the top.

Rhubarb Jelly, Ginger Ice Cream & Pistachios

This may sound like a cliché, but we were sitting drinking ginger tea one day when Tom came up with the idea for this dessert. The ginger ice cream goes so well with rhubarb gelatin.

You will need four ⅔-cup [150-ml] molds or ramekins.

SERVES 4

For the gelatin
1¾ cups [750 g] rhubarb, cut into
   2-in [5-cm] lengths
Juice of ½ orange
⅔ cup [125 g] sugar
3 sheets gelatin

For the ice cream
1¼ cups [300 ml] milk
1¼ cups [300 ml] whipping cream
½ cup [100 g] sugar
16 egg yolks
¼ cup [40 g] crystalized ginger, chopped
   into small dice

To serve
⅔ cup [80 g] pistachios, warmed in a
   dry frying pan and lightly crushed

Place the rhubarb, orange juice, and sugar in a pan with 1⅔ cups [400 ml] cold water and place over medium-low heat. Simmer for about 15 minutes, or until the rhubarb is soft. Give it a little whisk and then strain it through a fine-mesh sieve—don't force it through, just let it drain at its own pace; otherwise you'll have a cloudy jelly. This will take an hour or so.

Once drained, pour the strained juice into a measuring cup—you should have about 2½ cups [600 ml]. Place in a pan, return to the heat and bring up to a simmer, then turn off the heat.

Meanwhile, soak the gelatin in a bowl of cold water for 5 minutes to soften it. Once softened, squeeze out any excess water and then whisk the gelatin into your warm juice. Divide equally among your four molds and allow to cool slightly. Place in the fridge and allow to set for 8 hours or overnight.

To make the ice cream, heat the milk and cream together over medium heat until it starts to bubble around the edges, then remove the pan from the heat.

Using a balloon whisk, whisk the sugar and egg yolks together until thick and frothy; this will take about 8 minutes. Slowly pour the hot milk and cream into the egg mixture, whisking as you go.

Once everything is mixed together, pour the mixture into a clean pan and place over medium heat. Cook the custard for about 5 minutes, stirring continuously, until the custard starts to thicken. As soon as it's thick enough to coat the back of a spoon, pour the mixture into a container, allow to cool, and then put into the fridge.

Once the custard is completely cool, stir in the diced crystalized ginger and then pour the mixture into your ice cream maker. Churn, following the manufacturer's instructions.

Once churned, transfer to a suitable container and freeze for at least 3 hours before serving. If you don't have an ice cream maker, pour the mixture into a shallow container and place in the freezer; after an hour remove from the freezer and use a fork or whisk to break up the ice crystals. Return to the freezer and repeat this process every 30 minutes until the ice cream is smooth and creamy (you may need to do this four or five times). When your ice cream is fully churned, let it set in the freezer for at least 3 hours before serving.

When you are ready to serve, have a pan of hot water at the ready. Dip the gelatin molds into the hot water for no more than 2 seconds, just to loosen them. Turn the gelatins out onto individual plates and serve each with two scoops of ginger ice cream. Finish with a sprinkling of pistachios.

Poached Peaches, Sauternes & Mascarpone

A good peach is like a good fig: when you find one you shouldn't really do anything to it, just enjoy that soft, juicy, sweet flesh. Of course, it's not always easy to find perfection in a peach, but this dish will excuse any that are slightly less than perfect. Try to choose peaches that have dark skins and are still a little firm, with a lovely peachy scent.

SERVES 4
4 large peaches
¼ cup [50 g] granulated sugar
3 tbsp water
½ cup [100 ml] Sauternes
½ cup [100 ml] heavy cream
Zest of 1 lemon
2 tbsp confectioners' sugar
¾ cup [200 g] mascarpone

Preheat the oven to 350°F [180°C].

Use a sharp knife to cut the peaches in half, working your way around the pit. Twist the two halves to separate them, remove the pit, and then lay them cut-side up in a roasting pan.

Combine the granulated sugar, water, and Sauternes in a pan and cook over medium heat for a few minutes, or until the sugar has dissolved. Pour this over the peaches, cover them tightly with foil, and bake for 10 minutes. Remove from the oven, take off the foil, turn the peaches over, and allow them to cool in the juice.

Place the cream in a bowl and grate in the lemon zest. Add the confectioners' sugar and then whisk until soft peaks form (you can do this using a handheld electric mixer or by hand with a balloon whisk). Fold in the mascarpone and set aside.

When the peaches are cool enough to handle, peel off the skins and place them on a serving platter. Spoon the juices over them and finish with a dollop of the mascarpone cream.

This is a quick introduction to pickling, salting, and curing, and we've thrown in a few fermenting recipes too. We are also big on homemade drinks that use preserved fruits as their base, so you'll find recipes for some interesting drinks here too.

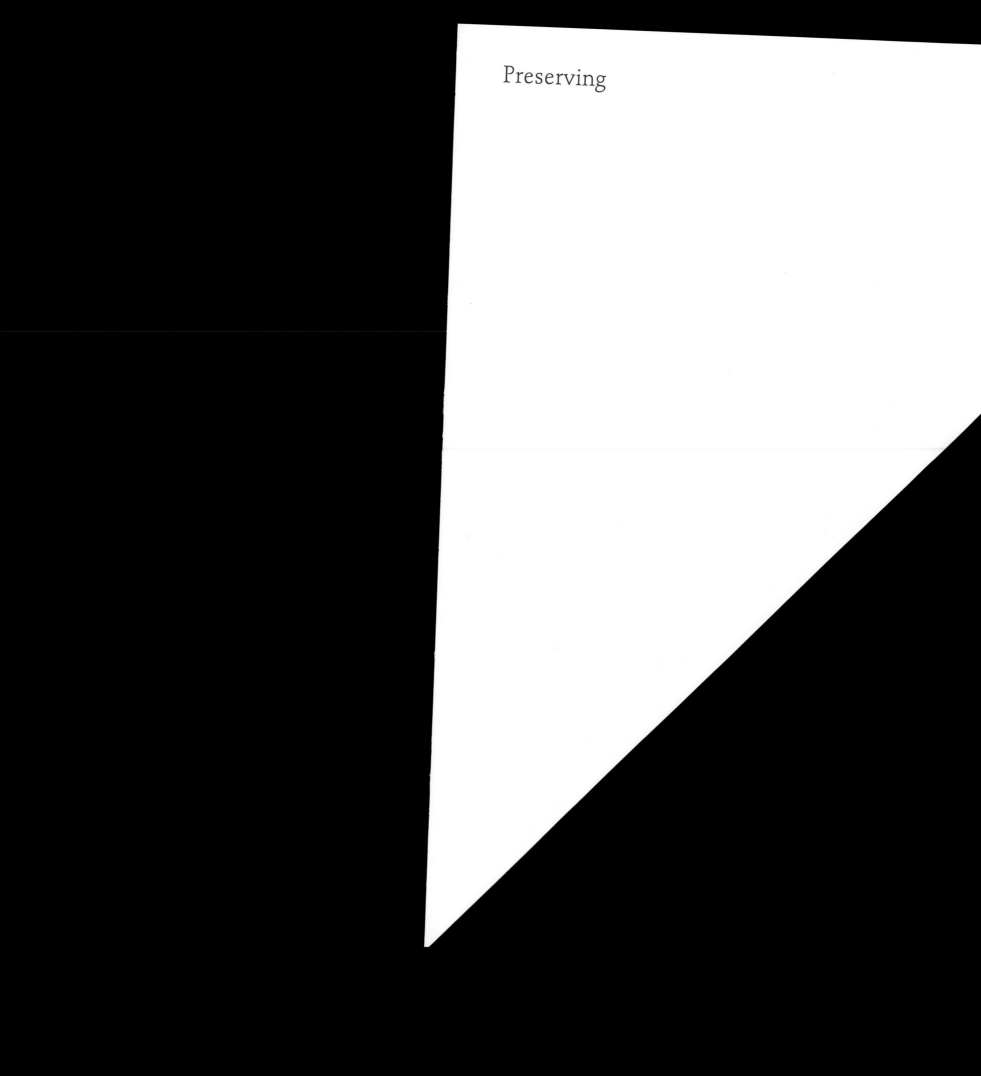

Preserving

Pickling

Pickling, fermenting, and preserving is something we're really interested in at both Ducksoup and our Hackney restaurant, Rawduck. It's about taking ingredients to the next level in order to bring a dish together or adding a different dimension. It uses very natural processes to intensify the flavors of raw ingredients, which is something we celebrate at Rawduck.

Pickled Vegetables

The art of pickling is nothing new. It has been a way of preserving food for centuries all over the world. When there was no refrigeration, the best way to store your food was to either pickle, salt, or smoke it to make it last through the colder months.

At the restaurant we always have a market pickle of sorts on the bar menu—we treat it like a sort of "bread and butter pickle,"—pickles so good that you can just eat them on your bread and butter.

Always try to use vegetables in good condition—we usually go for a box of something interesting and good value from our vegetable supplier, whether fennel, romanesco, cauliflower, or kohlrabi. We use a basic pickling recipe (see right) and then add different spices or herbs to complement whatever we are pickling.

Pickling is such a rewarding thing to do, and a great way to experiment with different vegetables. It also means you can use all the vegetable, so if you have half a cabbage left over or a surplus of cucumber or even a pumpkin that needs using up, you'll be able to fill a few mason jars with some lovely pickles, as a little goes a long way. If you are pickling something like cauliflower, then don't forget to use the leaves, ribs, and core of the cauliflower— the point of pickling is to not waste anything! We often pickle vegetable stems and call them "pickled ribs." And yes, people have ordered them expecting ribs.

Always make sure, once jarred, that your pickles are completely covered—we use a disk of parchment paper on the top of the liquid so that no air can get in. And always use clean, sterilized jars (see page 43).

Basic vegetable pickle

1 lb [500 g] vegetables
1 cup [250 ml] cider vinegar
1 cup [250 ml] water
¼ cup [50 g] superfine sugar
1 tsp sea salt
1 tsp black peppercorns
1 tsp fennel seeds

First prepare your vegetables. Cut into similar-sized pieces—too large and they'll take longer to pickle; too small and you'll miss out on that crunch. Aim for around ⅜-in [1-cm] pieces, but remember that like most of the things we do, you don't need perfectly straight cuts. Cut at an odd angle to add more texture and shape to your pickles.

Don't be afraid to make a mixed batch of something, so for example, radish and cucumbers go well together with the addition of a few dill fronds. Or try adding orange slices and dried chile flakes to some pickled fennel. Add some fresh green chile when pickling cabbage, which makes for an exciting little hit, or some fenugreek seeds and garam masala for a little Indian pickle.

Divide the prepared vegetables evenly among sterilized mason jars (see page 43). Warm the remaining ingredients together in a large pan to dissolve the sugar, allow it to cool, and then pour over the prepared vegetables.

Add a circle of parchment paper to the top of each jar and add the lid. Store in a cool, dry place for up to 2 months.

Pickled Fruits

You can also have a lot of fun pickling fruit, and we do this when we have a surplus of fruit such as pears, plums, rhubarb, or grapes. The basic recipe is slightly different, with more sugar. Fruit pickles pair well with savory foods such as cheese or fattier meats like pork (see the recipe for Slow-roasted Pork Belly & Pickled Rhubarb on page 201).

Basic sweet pickle
1 lb [500 g] fruit
2½ cups [500 g] superfine sugar
1 cup [250 ml] cider vinegar
1 cup [250 ml] water
Spices (optional)

First prepare the fruit, removing any pits and cutting into ⅜-in [1-cm] pieces. Add to your sterilized mason jars (see page 43).

Warm the sugar, vinegar, and water together in a pan until the sugar dissolves. Add whatever spices you fancy, such as cardamom and star anise for rhubarb, a cinnamon stick and dried chile for grapes, or bay leaves, fennel seeds, and star anise for plums.

Allow to cool before pouring the pickling liquid over the fruits. Add a circle of parchment paper to the top of each jar and add the lid. Store in an airtight container in the fridge for up to 1 week.

Pickled rhubarb

You'll find a lot of rhubarb in this book—it lends itself to many dishes, not just desserts but also meat dishes and, of course, drinks. We prefer to use the early-season rhubarb, which is a vibrant pink and so makes for pretty dishes. When the outdoor season comes around in summer months, the rhubarb is less pink and, once cooked, takes on a muddy brown pink color, which is not as beautiful. But it can't be all about a pretty face, so of course we continue to cook with rhubarb—we just use it in different ways.

2¼ cups [250 g] superfine sugar
1 cup [250 ml] cider vinegar
½ cup [100 ml] water
4 green cardamom pods, lightly crushed
1 star anise
Pinch of dried chile flakes
1 lb [500 g] early-forced rhubarb, cut into
    2-in [5-cm] pieces

Put the sugar, vinegar, water, and spices in a pan and bring to a gentle simmer, then cook for about 5 minutes.

Drop the rhubarb pieces into the pan in batches and cook for 30 to 45 seconds, or until you see the rhubarb change to a much paler color. Remove immediately with a slotted spoon and allow to cool flat on a baking pan. Repeat this process until all the rhubarb is cooked.

Allow the liquid to cool and then pour it over the rhubarb. If you pour it over while it is still hot, you will overcook the rhubarb.

Store the rhubarb in an airtight container in the fridge for a couple of weeks. Delicious with a good piece of mature Cheddar.

Quick Pickles

If you like the idea of pickling but don't have much time, then try *tsukemono*—it's a Japanese term meaning "impatient pickles" or "quick pickles." Here are two of our favorite quick pickle recipes, including one that is super quick, as it doesn't require salting.

Watermelon radish

Watermelon radish is a Chinese radish with a pale green exterior and wonderful pink flesh, hence the watermelon reference. You can use breakfast radishes instead, or even turnips. We use this in the recipe for Chopped Raw Hanger Steak, Pickled Radish & Ricotta Salata (see page 95).

4 oz [100 g] watermelon radish
Pinch of salt
3 tbsp cider vinegar
1½ tsp water
2 tsp sugar

Cut off the top and bottom of the radish and then cut in half across. Using a mandoline, thinly slice the radish into a bowl. Add a pinch of salt and then use your hands to massage it into the radish for about 2 minutes to encourage the radish to release some of its natural juice.

In a separate bowl, mix together the vinegar, water, and sugar until the sugar has dissolved. Pour over the radish and leave to pickle for 3 hours. Store in an airtight container in the fridge for up to 1 week.

Wood ear mushrooms

These are delicious fresh pickles to enliven your taste buds at the beginning of your meal and could not be quicker to make.

4 oz [100 g] dried wood ear mushrooms
¾ cup [175 ml] chinkiang vinegar
1 tbsp sesame oil
⅓ cup [75 ml] soy sauce
1 green chile, chopped
1 tbsp toasted sesame seeds
1 tbsp light brown sugar
1 small onion, preferably spring,
   thinly sliced
Pinch of salt

Place the dried mushrooms in a pan and cover with cold water. Leave to soak for 15 minutes, then place over medium-high heat and bring to a boil. Simmer for 2 minutes, then drain and refresh in ice water.

Remove and discard the stalks from the mushrooms and then add the mushrooms to a bowl with the remaining ingredients. Mix to combine. The pickle will be ready to eat immediately, but will keep in the fridge for a couple of days.

Dairy

As for Labneh (page 323), making your own fresh dairy couldn't be simpler, and the taste is worth the effort.

Goat's curd

Goat's curd is made when you separate the milk solids from the whey, resulting in a creamy, fresh cheese that can be eaten on its own or used in recipes. Made from fresh goats milk and salt by a gentle process, it adds a subtle tang and sweetness to many dishes throughout this book.

4¼ cups [1 L] goats milk
2 tsp lemon juice or white vinegar

In a large saucepan, warm the milk to 97°F [36°C]. Stir in the lemon juice or vinegar and let the mixture rest for 30 minutes at room temperature. Put the mixture back over low heat, stirring occasionally, until it reaches 194°F [90°C]. Remove from the heat and let the mixture rest for 30 minutes.

Line a fine-mesh sieve with cheesecloth or a large coffee filter and set it over a large bowl. Pour the mixture into the sieve and leave to strain for 1 hour, allowing separaton of the curds from the whey. Use curd immediately or store in an airtight container in the fridge for up to 3 days.

Ferments

At Rawduck we're more adventurous with our preserving—
here we're also very much into fermenting. We make our own
kimchi, which is a Korean method of fermenting and preserving,
traditionally using Chinese cabbage, Korean chile flakes, ginger,
garlic, soy, and fish sauce.

We use our basic recipe with a variety of different vegetables, such
as fennel, kohlrabi, Brussels sprouts—even cauliflower stems,
which so often just get thrown away.

Fermented foods have been eaten for centuries for their probiotics,
creating good gut flora and helping your digestive system to
absorb nutrients from your food. Be warned, your fermenting
foods will let off a bit of a funky smell from time to time, but
that's all part of nature's process.

Kohlrabi kimchi

The vegetable is either shredded or cut into bite-sized pieces, salted for 24 hours, mixed with the rest of the kimchi blend, and then left to ferment for a few weeks. We have shelves of different vegetables fermenting and bubbling away—each jar with its own ecosystem. It's fascinating.

MAKES ABOUT 4½ LB [2 KG]
4½ lb [2 kg] kohlrabi
1 tbsp salt
2 tbsp sugar
6 large garlic cloves, grated
One 5- to 6-inch piece [100 g] fresh ginger, peeled and grated
1 cup [250 ml] light soy sauce
1 cup [250 ml] fish sauce
2 tbsp Gochugaru or dried chile flakes

Finely slice the kohlrabi using a mandoline, and add to a bowl with the salt and sugar. Rub the ingredients together so that you start to release some of the water, and then tip into a colander set over a bowl and leave overnight to release more water.

The following day, briefly rinse in cold water and drain.

Mix the garlic, ginger, soy sauce, fish sauce, and chile flakes together and then rub into the drained kohlrabi. Pack into sterilized mason jars (see page 43), leaving ⅜ in [1 cm] of space at the top. Close your lid and leave to ferment for a least 1 week before using. As with all ferments and pickles, don't ferment them in direct sunlight; store in a dark place but nowhere too cold. As they begin to ferment, liquid might seep out of the top, so place them on a small saucer to collect any juices. Once opened, store in the fridge for up to a month.

Sauerkraut

A simple first fermentation—all you need to do is salt your cabbage and then the natural bacteria starts to ferment and break the cabbage down. It's then preserved in its own brine made from the salt and cabbage water. We rub the sea salt into the vegetable pieces, which breaks them down, and then pack it all into a fermenting crock or mason jar. It will immediately start to release liquid, so you need to weigh it down with a disk of parchment paper—you don't want it exposed to the air. A traditional fermenting crock comes with its own weight, but if you are not using one of these use a non-metallic plate. And now all you need to do is let nature take its course. The process will start to happen within 2 days, but it's best to give it about a month to fully ferment.

MAKES ABOUT 4 CUPS [1 L]
1 head white or red cabbage
1 tbsp fine sea salt
4 tsp caraway seeds

Thinly shred the cabbage using a mandoline. Rub the salt into the cabbage so that you start to release the natural water from the cabbage. At this point taste it for salt—it should be salty but not unpleasantly so.

Add the caraway seeds and pack into your crock or fermenting jar. Weigh down and leave in a cool dark place (not the fridge) for 2 days. If after 2 days the cabbage is not submerged in the brine, then add a little salted water to top it up.

Leave to ferment for at least 2 weeks, ideally for a full month. Once opened, store in the fridge for up to a month.

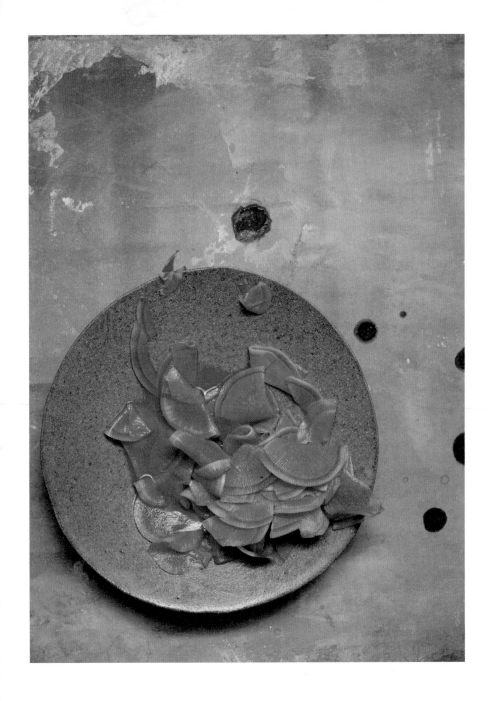

Salting

Another traditional way of preserving food is salting, which we do quite a bit at both restaurants. It's a method used mainly to cure fish, but also meats, such as prosciutto, guanciale, and pancetta—charcuterie that we use a lot of. (You can read more about the types of charcuterie we use in On Charcuterie & Cheese on page 113). These recipes are all salt-cured for different lengths of time and with different herbs and spices to give them their unique flavors. However, this section also covers salting other foods, such as salt-preserved lemons and labneh (salted Greek yogurt).

We like to use Cornish sea salt in our cooking, first, because it's saltier than other sea salts, meaning you use less, and second, because it only takes a small portion of the salt from the sea water.

Salt-Cured Cod

We've used salt cod in a couple of recipes in this book (Salt Cod, Tomato & Olive Oil, page 59, and Salt Cod, Blood Orange, Fennel & Chile, page 69). At the restaurant we usually salt a whole cod, but if you are making this at home you can salt a much smaller piece. Buy from your local fishmonger and make sure you get a skinned piece cut from the thick end of a large cod fillet. A small, thin fillet won't give you the same texture and the curing time will be different from that stated below.

14-oz [400-g] piece of cod fillet, cut from the thick end and skinned
¾ cup [200 g] sea salt

Spread half the salt out in the bottom of a nonmetallic pan or shallow dish. Place the cod fillet on top and then cover with the remaining salt. Leave in the fridge to cure for 10 hours (you can either do this the night before or first thing in the morning, so it's ready by the end of the day). However, don't cure for more than 10 hours.

After the curing time you will see that a lot of water has been drawn from the fish and that the fish itself has firmed up. Rinse the fish and cut off a slice to see how salty it is. If it's too salty, then immerse the fillet in a bowl of ice water for 30 minutes and then test again. The fish should be pleasantly salty and firm to the taste. Pat dry with paper towels and store in the fridge, either wrapped in plastic wrap or in an airtight container, for up to 5 days.

Use in one of the recipes mentioned at left; alternatively you can just slice it and serve with some very thinly sliced red onion, a generous drizzle of extra-virgin olive oil, a squeeze of lemon juice, and some torn flat-leaf parsley. What more could you want?

Labneh

Labneh is an ingredient that appears again and again on our menu and throughout this book. It's salted and strained Greek yogurt, almost a sort of yogurt cheese. A staple item in Middle Eastern cooking, it's really easy to make and it's ideal to have a small batch in the fridge because it's so versatile. It's also just delicious spread on crusty sourdough with fresh herbs and lashings of good extra-virgin olive oil.

But there are other great ways to use it. It's perfect served alongside some grilled meat, as a cooler to a spicy slow cook, or as a large spoonful on the side of roast vegetables with a sprinkle of toasted sesame seeds and sea salt.

At home you'll want a smaller quantity, so as a rule simply whisk 1 tsp salt into every 2 cups [500 g] full-fat natural Greek yogurt (don't be tempted to use a fat-free version, as it won't be the same). Pour the mixture into cheesecloth suspended over a bowl (you can also use a large coffee filter) to allow the excess liquid to drip through. Depending how thick you want your labneh, leave it overnight for medium-firm or 3 days for super-firm.

Labneh under oil

If you leave your labneh for 3 days it will become firm enough to roll into small balls. You can then preserve them in olive oil and herbs. Simply add the balls to a jar and pour over enough extra-virgin olive oil to cover them. Tear in plenty of fresh herbs (chives, dill, flat-leaf parsley, chervil) and that's it! Dip into the jar at any time of day—the labneh is delicious spread on charred sourdough.

Lime pickle

We serve this lime pickle with crumpets and Cheddar on our breakfast menu—it's a good little number to get your taste buds into gear.

2 lb [1 kg] limes
2 tbsp coarse sea salt
2 tbsp sugar
⅔ cup [150 ml] mustard oil
3 tbsp mustard seeds
3 tbsp cayenne pepper
1 tbsp fenugreek seeds
3 tbsp ground turmeric

Cut the limes in half from top to bottom but don't cut all the way through, then turn the lime 45 degrees and cut from top to bottom again, again making sure you don't cut all the way through. You want your slices to remain joined at one end. Pack them with the salt and sugar into mason jars, squashing well. Seal the lids, shake, and leave to ferment for 1 month.

After that time, heat the oil and spices in a pan over low heat for a few minutes. Add the fermented limes along with all their juice and cook for 5 minutes. Allow to cool and then pack into fresh mason jars. Store for 1 week before using, and after opening keep in the fridge for up to 2 months.

Preserves

We also use the salt-curing method to make our own preserved lemons and oranges. It's a cross between salt curing and fermenting. While the lemons or oranges are preserving in their own brine, they take on a completely different flavor and texture.

Preserved lemons

This is an old Middle Eastern way of keeping lemons long after they are picked. The only difficult thing is having the patience to wait the 2 to 3 months until they are ready. But they are worth the wait and it only take a few minutes to assemble a jar. Make up a big batch so you have a good stock, and remember that when you open the last jar, it's time to start preserving more.

2 lb [1 kg] organic unwaxed lemons
About ¾ cup [250 g] coarse sea salt

Cut the lemons in half from top to bottom, but don't cut all the way through, then turn the lemon 45 degrees and cut from top to bottom again, again making sure you don't cut all the way through. You want your slices to remain joined at one end.

Holding the lemons over a bowl, pack some salt into the cut parts of the lemon. Push the whole lemons firmly into a sterilized mason jar (see page 43). Continue this process with the rest of the lemons,

packing them into the jar as tightly as possible. You may need to cut a few in half in order to fill any gaps.

Once all the lemons are packed in, fill the jars with filtered water, or water that has been boiled (and cooled). Add any remaining salt and juice that has fallen into the bowl. You can, if you like, add a couple of cinnamon sticks or cardamom pods and even a pinch of dried chile flakes or whole dried chiles. Once everything that needs to go into the jar is tightly packed in, tuck a disk of parchment paper over the top to make sure that everything is submerged. Close your jar lid and give it all a good shake. Leave somewhere cool and out of direct sunlight to do its thing. Check the jars once a week, giving them a shake to help the salt to dissolve.

After 2 to 3 months they'll be ready to enjoy. Thinly slice the lemons, mix with chile, toasted cumin, coriander, and mint, and serve as a salad with meat, fish, or slow-cooked lamb shoulder, or try the Grilled Quail, Mograbiah & Preserved Lemon (page 150).

Preserved oranges

Lucy Pearce, who used to work with us at Rawduck, also preserved some oranges with rosemary, which were beautiful. Preserve as for lemons, adding whole rosemary sprigs to the jars once you have packed in the oranges.

Curing

Curing is similar to salting, but here the addition of aromatics gives it more flavor and depth, where salting is literally just adding salt. Our cured salmon recipe is based on the Nordic recipe for gravlax and will take 3 days to cure, so do bear this in mind. One of our favorite recipes in this book is Cured Salmon, Buttermilk, Shaved Radish & Dill (page 54). It might seem like an effort to cure the salmon for just one dish, but there are plenty of ways you can gobble up any leftovers. It's delicious with scrambled eggs, of course, but also in a quick salad, with parsley, capers, radishes, and dill.

Cured salmon

1¼ cups [350 g] table salt
¾ cup [150 g] sugar
Handful of mint leaves
Handful of dill leaves
1⅓ lb [600 g] skin-on salmon fillet cut
    from the fat end, pin-boned

First make the cure by blending the salt, sugar, and herbs in a food processor for 1 minute. If you don't have a food processor you can finely chop the herbs by hand and then mix everything together in a large bowl.

Cut the salmon fillet into two pieces. Roll out a double layer of plastic wrap, about 3 ft [1 m] long, on your work surface. Spread a quarter of the cure on the plastic at one end, about the length of one of the salmon pieces. Lay a piece of salmon, skin-side down, on top of the cure.

Spread two-thirds of the remaining cure on the flesh-side of the salmon. Lay the other fillet skin-side up and the opposite way around, so that the tail is on the fat-side of the other fillet. Spread the remaining cure over the skin-side of the top fillet.

Tightly wrap the salmon in the plastic wrap, as tight as it will go, wrapping around until all the plastic wrap is used up. Place on a nonmetallic dish (this will collect any liquid that is drawn out by the salt) and place in the fridge with a gentle weight on top—a plate is ideal.

Turn the salmon over a couple of times a day, once in the morning and once at night. This means the salmon will get an even cure, rather than one side curing more than the other. You'll see the moisture coming out of the salmon after a day; this will create its own brine that then helps it cure.

After 3 or 4 days the salmon will be ready. Unwrap the plastic wrap, give the salmon a quick rinse under a cold tap to remove some of the salt cure, and then pat dry with paper towels.

The cured salmon will keep for up to 5 days in the fridge. To serve, thinly slice with a sharp knife. You can also cut it into small dice and stir into scrambled eggs.

Drinks

Many of our drinks are homemade—Rory is our drinks maker. It's important to us that our drinks also reflect the way we cook and our approach to ingredients and cooking. In the same way that we talk about our menus and what we'd like to eat, we share thoughts on what we'd like to drink, but he's the one that gets into the kitchen and experiments to create the perfect recipe. Like the food on our menu, our drinks are seasonal, and they change as often as the food. Flavors and unusual touches excite us and make all the difference, whether it's rhubarb pulp or vanilla seeds, the fresh thyme in our lemon cordial or the lemon zest we add to our cold brew coffee.

We've provided rough quantities for all our drink recipes, but please note that quantity will vary according to the ripeness of the fruit you're using.

Shrubs

A shrub is an old-fashioned way of preserving fruit, similar to pickling. Shrubs gained popularity in the 19th century. The fruit was traditionally mixed with vinegar to create a syrup that forms the basis of a soft drink or a cocktail. We use this method to create the base for fruit drinks, cocktails, and our drinking vinegars. Here are a few of our favorite shrub recipes. You can add sparkling wine such as prosecco, cava, or even champagne to these, use them as a fruit base for a cocktail, or simply enjoy with sparkling water and ice.

Apricot shrub

MAKES 2 CUPS [½ L]
1 lb [500 g] apricots
2½ cups [500 g] turbinado sugar
1¼ cups [300 ml] filtered water
½ vanilla pod, seeds scraped out
5 bay leaves
¾ cup [200 ml] apple cider vinegar
Sparkling wine, to serve

Rinse the fruit under the tap, then remove the pits and cut the flesh into small pieces. Add to a pan with the sugar, water, vanilla (seeds and pod), and bay leaves and bring to a boil. Reduce the heat to a steady simmer and cook for 45 minutes to 1 hour, or until the fruit is soft and cooked and the syrup has been infused with all the flavors.

Leave to cool overnight. Then add the vinegar and leave, covered, on the side, for a further 24 hours. The following day pour into a sieve suspended over a bowl and leave for a few hours—you want to make sure you get all of that syrup, and the extraction can't be rushed. The shrubs can be stored in the fridge for up to 3 months.

To serve, pour about 2 tbsp of the syrup into a glass (champagne or wine, it's up to you) and top with sparkling wine (or use 1 part syrup to 4 parts sparkling wine).

Spiced sparkling quince shrub

We celebrate quinces in the same way that we do bergamot—for some reason both of these fruits make us think of more indulgent or exotic times; perhaps it's because they often appear in oil paintings of grand feasts from the 18th and 19th centuries. The quince season is a small one, and somehow marks a time of rich givings, maybe because it signals that Christmas is just around the corner. We like to use quince in desserts but also in this lovely shrub that Rory created for us.

MAKES 4 CUPS [1 L]
4 large quince, peeled, cored, and cut into eighths
1½ cups [300 g] turbinado sugar
One 5-inch [90-g] piece fresh ginger, thinly sliced
4 star anise, smashed with a pestle and mortar
Juice of 2 lemons (preferably organic), sieved
10½ cups [2.5 L] filtered water
2¼ cups [500 ml] apple cider vinegar

Combine all the ingredients together in a large pan and slowly bring to a boil. Reduce the heat and simmer for 20 minutes. Be careful to not let the fruit go limp; you want it to retain a little bite. Turn off the heat, cover the pan, and leave overnight to infuse. The next day add the vinegar and leave, covered, on the side, for a further 24 hours.

The following day strain the liquid through a sieve set over a bowl. Discard the spices but keep the fruit—it makes a delicious breakfast with yogurt. Taste the liquid— if you find that the flavor is not strong enough, you can always return it to a pan and simmer over a steady heat to reduce to a thicker consistency.

Store in a glass bottle in the fridge for at least 1 month before drinking. It will keep for up to 3 months in the fridge.

Drinking Vinegars

Drinking vinegars are slowly becoming popular again; they have a great history in terms of good health, as unpasteurized vinegar is said to be very good for the digestive system, helping it to absorb all the essential nutrients in our diet.

Raspberry drinking vinegar soda

This is made in a similar way to a shrub, but unpasteurized vinegar is added, preserving the fruit as well as adding goodness (unpasteurized vinegar is a live fermentation and therefore full of probiotics).

1½ lb [650 g] raspberries, washed
1⅔ cups [325 g] turbinado sugar
1½ cups [375 ml] raw unpasteurized apple cider vinegar (look for one that says it contains "mother" on the label)

Combine the raspberries and sugar in a large bowl and mash together with a wooden spoon. Cover with a lid (or plastic wrap) and leave to macerate for 48 hours.

Decant the mixture into a sterilized mason jar (see page 43), add the vinegar, and seal the lid. Store in the fridge for 5 to 10 days. During this period the ingredients are getting to know each other, so you need to taste daily (stir gently, as jars can easily break when cold). When tasting you're looking for a good balance of acidity, tart fruit and a mellowness from the sugar. (The sugar is only there to knock our some of the tartness—you want the fruit to taste more of itself, rather than being overly sweet.) If it does just that, then you're ready to strain; if not, return to the fridge to carry on developing.

Make a little bag with a square of muslin, tying all four ends together. Hang over a bowl suspended from a butcher's hook (pictured opposite) and tip in the fruit and liquid. When the pulp inside the muslin bag is dry, you can add a small handful back to the liquid to give it some texture.

To serve, pour 3 to 5 tbsp [50 to 75 ml] of the vinegar syrup into a tumbler full of ice cubes. Top with sparkling water.

Rhubarb shrub and drinking vinegar

We love rhubarb and use it in drinks as well as in our cooking, particularly early-forced rhubarb, which has great color, sweetness and acidity. We make drinking vinegars from this and also use it as the base for one of our shrubs. Both go down very well.

2 lb [1 kg] early-forced rhubarb, cut into ⅜-in [1-cm] pieces
2½ cups [500 g] turbinado sugar
1⅔ cups [400 ml] raw unpasteurized apple cider vinegar
1⅔ cups [400 ml] filtered water
1 large vanilla bean
1¼ oz [35 g] green cardamom pods, lightly crushed

In a large saucepan over medium-low heat, combine the rhubarb, sugar, vinegar and water. Split the vanilla bean lengthwise and use a knife to carefully scrape the seeds into the pan. Stir immediately so that they separate rather than clump together.

Remove the black seeds from the crushed cardamom pods and dry fry over medium heat for no more than 20 seconds to release the oils. Add the seeds to the pan and slowly bring to a boil. Reduce the heat and simmer for about 15 minutes. $\rightarrow$

Allow to cool completely and then pour into a clean sterilized mason jar (see page 43). Seal and place in the fridge. Leave for 5 to 10 days to let the flavors infuse. Taste it every day to see how it changes and when it is ready. You're looking for a balance of sweetness, tart fruit, and acidity.

When it tastes right you're ready to strain. Make a little bag with a square of muslin, tying all four ends together. Hang over a bowl and tip in the fruit and liquid. You're looking for an almost clear liquid, so this process is best done overnight. You can help it along buy squeezing and squashing the pulp, but it's not a process you can rush.

When you've got a clear liquid, take a small handful of the soft pink fruit (making sure you get a few vanilla seeds) and whisk into the liquid; discard the remaining pulp. This will add a pretty pinkness to the drink, but it will settle at the bottom, so always shake before using.

To serve, pour 3 to 5 tbsp [50 to 75 ml] of the rhubarb vinegar syrup into a tumbler full of ice cubes. Top with sparkling water. Alternatively, pour about 2 tbsp into a champagne flute or wineglass and top with sparkling wine (prosecco works best here).

Green Gooseberry Pisco Sour

This is Rory's recipe for a Pisco Sour. He loves gooseberries and greengages for their tartness and so experimented by putting them in a Pisco Sour. Pisco Sour was something our customers kept asking for, and we just couldn't bring ourselves to put it on the menu unless we did it our way. So here it is. Gooseberries vary in their sugar levels throughout the season, so when making the syrup do taste and adjust your recipe accordingly.

MAKES ENOUGH FOR 2–3 PISCO SOURS
For the gooseberry syrup
10 oz [300 g] tart green gooseberries (ideally slightly underripe, so not too soft)
½ cup [100 g] turbinado sugar

First make the syrup. If your gooseberries are on the riper side, double the amount of gooseberries and reduce the sugar quantity to taste.

Combine the gooseberries and sugar in a bowl and use the end of a rolling pin to mash together. You want to really combine all that skin and juice with the sugar. Leave covered in the fridge for 2 to 3 days, giving it a bash with the rolling pin every day.

When you think that you have extracted as much liquid as possible from the berries, it's ready. It should still taste tart and not too sweet. Strain in a conical sieve set over a bowl, pressing really hard to extract all the juice from the skin and pulp. You'll be left with a clear liquid, but you can add a few seeds for aesthetic value. Decant into a sterilized bottle (see page 43), ready to make your Pisco Sours.

SERVES 1
3 tbsp gooseberry syrup (see above)
2 tbsp nonaromatic Pisco (we like 1615 de Gran Terruño)
1 tsp lemon juice, sieved
½ small egg white
2 dashes Amargo Chunco bitters (optional)

To make a Pisco Sour, pour 3 tbsp of your gooseberry syrup into a cocktail shaker. Add the remaining ingredients, together with a good handful of ice, and shake a couple of times (you don't want to shake for too long or the ice will melt and dilute the cocktail). Strain into a pretty glass, ideally one with a long stem. Enjoy.

Lebanese White Coffee

Although this is not a coffee as such, Tom came across this recipe and thought it would be great to serve some of those pretty blossomed waters in a drink at Rawduck. So if you are seeking a caffeine hit, this is not your drink. This is more of a hot perfumed water, but it's delicious and cleansing.

2 tbsp orange blossom water
1 tsp honey or unrefined sugar
⅔ cup [150 ml] hot water, from a recently boiled kettle

Stir all the ingredients together in a glass and enjoy.

Kombucha

Kombucha is a fermented tea, and ancient tradition says it is very good for you and your gut flora, helping your digestive system to function properly. You will need a "SCOBY," which stands for symbiotic colony of bacteria and yeast—these can easily be purchased online.

1 cup plus 3 tbsp [235 g] turbinado sugar
3 qt plus 3 cups [3.5 L] boiling water
½ cup [35 g] loose-leaf tea (we use oolong but you can use green or other types, or mix in some black tea for more tannin)
1 SCOBY

Dissolve the sugar in the boiling water in a large pan, then add the tea and leave to cool completely. Strain the tea and decant the liquid into a crock or large glass jar that you can cover tightly with muslin. Making sure you have very clean hands, add your SCOBY—you don't want any nasty bacteria to get in—and avoid using metallic utensils. Leave to ferment in the crock for 7 to 10 days, during which time the bacteria will eat away all the sugar.

After this period taste the tea for the desired ratio of tart to sweet—this really is up to you, but you should be looking for just a little vinegary taste, but not too much. Follow the package instructions for using the SCOBY carefully—if you see any sign of black mold or the kombucha smells eggy, immediately discard the kombucha, as it means that your bacteria have taken a turn for the worse and will do you more harm than good.

Once you're happy with your fermented tea, you're ready to decant into sterilized bottles (see page 43), ideally with a capped top. At this point you can infuse your kombucha with a few hibiscus leaves, but remove them after a few days as they will go moldy.

Kombucha is alive and so is changing all the time as it goes through its fermentation process. It will therefore produce gases, and these do need to be let out. Otherwise, you could end up with exploding bottles all over your kitchen. So it's best to burp your bottled kombucha every couple of days, just like a baby. As with any fermenting foods, don't store in direct sunlight; similarly, don't put them in the coldest corner ever because they will just die. The kombucha will be ready after about 7 to 10 days.

Tool Kit

Because we believe in doing everything simply, we're not going to give you a long list of gadgets that you need in the kitchen, and we're not going to list everything you might use, because we're assuming your kitchen will be equipped with some basic utensils, from a metal spatula to a decent potato peeler.

However, there are a few pieces of equipment that we highly recommend to make both preparation and cooking easier. We hope these will become part of your cooking life; good knives and pans that are well looked after will last a lifetime and you'll become so used to cooking with them that it will be a pleasure to use them. Think of them as your good friends.

Knives

If you're investing in a good knife, then do seek advice from the store or read up about the brand or product—this really applies to anything that you want to last you a long time. It's a good idea to buy a set, and make sure you look after them as they really are a cook's best friend. If you don't have the right tool for the job, then you'll be starting on the back foot. Find knives that sit comfortably in your hand; this can be a very personal thing.

Ideally you should have one small knife and one medium-large knife, and make sure you keep them sharpened. Always use the right knife for the job—if you are peeling an artichoke, use a small knife, as you want to be close to the ingredient to turn it. Larger knives are more suited to chopping vegetables, cutting meat, or slicing raw fish. A 10-in [25-cm] knife is perfect for these jobs; any bigger and you won't have control over what you're doing.

Tongs

Tongs are invaluable in the kitchen, as they're needed for nearly all cooking jobs, whether turning meat, flipping shrimp, serving pasta, or gently lifting a salad out of a bowl to drop onto a plate. As with a good knife, you will become attached to a good set of tongs because they have so many uses. After a while you'll be lost without them.

Microplane grater

This is another utensil that everyone should have. Find one that has a fine grater; if it's too large you won't end up with the clean zest of a lemon, or you will get big chunks of garlic going into your garlic yogurt, instead of a near purée. These are also very handy for grating cheese like Parmesan and for finely grating ricotta salata.

Large cast-iron skillet and grill pan

When it comes to these two items, it really does pay to buy the best you can afford. A good grill pan should last forever, as long as it is well looked after.

Do a little research and choose a size of pan that suits your cooking. If you are mainly cooking for two, then a 12-in [30-cm] pan will be fine; any bigger and all you'll be doing is heating up a larger surface area that you don't need, and it's better to keep your cooking tight and in control. Having a larger one as well for when you are cooking for friends is a good idea.

A good-quality cast-iron grill pan is crucial to much of the cooking that we do. Please don't be tempted to buy some cheap nonstick thing. It will probably work fine a couple of times and then give up its nonstick coating and become useless. Instead buy cast iron, keep it clean and lightly oiled after use, and, most important, keep it dry to prevent rusting.

Mandoline

This really is an essential piece of equipment for us: it's the best, almost the only way to achieve elegant ribbons of whatever ingredient you are using. Our kitchen would be lost without one. And once you have mastered that little tweak that makes the blade cut the perfect thickness, you won't know how you managed before you had one. Don't think that this is some kind of cheat's gadget—the results are fast and, most importantly, consistent, and all the best cooks use them. You can find these in cookware shops and online, but watch your fingers and always use the blade guard!

Clare Lattin started her career in book publishing over 20 years ago with Hodder Headline; she then traveled the world for 18 months working in restaurants. On returning to the UK she fell back into publishing, most recently at Quadrille, where she worked for 10 years as head of publicity, overseeing all their major cookbooks. During this period her passion for the food scene became obsessive, and it was here that she met the characters who put her on the path to opening her own restaurant. Clare also is the cofounder of Eightyfour, a small PR agency specializing in restaurant and food brands. Most recently, she has launched a ceramic brand called "vessel and time."

Tom Hill's love of cooking began as a child in the kitchen with his mother. Today, as a professional chef, he is executive chef of Ducksoup and co-proprietor of Rawduck. Tom has worked with a number of leading lights in the restaurant industry. He has managed the kitchens for Mitch Tonks of Fish Works, Mark Hix of Hix Restaurants, and Ed Wilson of Terroir (now chef-proprietor of Brawn).

Acknowledgments

Our parents, grandparents, and siblings, in no particular order: Humphrey and Joan Lattin, Michael and Rebecca Hill, Eugene and Barbara McCoy, Mary-Clare McCoy, Jane Lattin, Rob and Nicola Hill for their inspiration and support and for introducing us to good food, encouraging us in whichever way to enjoy cooking, restaurants, and the infectious and happy experiences of sharing food together. Other members of our families, including uncles and aunts who worked their lives in restaurants, pubs, and grocery stores and instilled in us their values of conviviality and community through food.

Those who work hard to make Ducksoup and Rawduck the restaurants they are: Pete Dorman, Orlaith McKeever, Angel Bautista, Alex Coburn-Davis, and Jordan Rouye.

And all of the people we have worked with or watched and learned from—there are so many, but to name a few: Mark Hix, Mitch Tonks, Matt Prowse, Benny, Alison Cathie, Julian Biggs, Ratnesh Bagdai, Byron Lang, Seb Fogg, Jeremy King, and Mitch Everard.

Other thanks go to Declan Madigan, Guillaume Aubert, Phil Barnett, Ivan Mulcahy, Rowan Yapp, Kristin Perers, Tabitha Hawkins, A Practice for Everyday Life, Elliot from The Ham & Cheese Company, Daphne of Daphne's Lamb, Vittorio of Natoora, Brett Barnes, and Cinzia Ghignoni.

Index

First published in the United States in 2017 by Chronicle Books, LLC.
First published in the United Kingdom in 2016 by Square Peg.
Copyright © 2016 by Clare Lattin and Tom Hill.
Photography copyright © Kristin Perers.

Library of Congress Cataloging-in-Publication Data:

Names: Lattin, Clare, author. | Hill, Tom, 1979- author.
Title: Ducksoup : the wisdom of simple cooking / Clare Lattin and Tom Hill.
Description: San Francisco : Chronicle Books, [2017] | Includes index.
Identifiers: LCCN 2016031797 | ISBN 9781452161792 (hc : alk. paper)
Subjects: LCSH: Quick and easy cooking. | Cooking, Scandinavian. | Cooking,
    Mediterranean. | Ducksoup (Restaurant)
Classification: LCC TX833.5 .L377 2017 | DDC 641.5/12--dc23 LC record
available at https://lccn.loc.gov/2016031797

ISBN: 978-1-4521-6179-2

Manufactured in China.

Photography by Kristin Perers
Design and art direction by A Practice for Everyday Life
Props styling by Tabitha Hawkins
Food styling by Tom Hill

10 9 8 7 6 5 4 3 2 1

Chronicle Books LLC
680 Second Street
San Francisco, CA 94107
www.chroniclebooks.com